Air Safety

Preventing Future Disasters

Air Safety
Preventing Future Disasters

Timothy R. Gaffney

Enslow Publishers, Inc.

40 Industrial Road	PO Box 38
Box 398	Aldershot
Berkeley Heights, NJ 07922	Hants GU12 6BP
USA	UK

http://www.enslow.com

Library of Congress Cataloging-in-Publication Data

Gaffney, Timothy R.
    Air safety : preventing future disasters / Timothy R. Gaffney.
        p. cm. — (Issues in focus)
    Includes index.
    Summary: Traces the history of air safety, discussing air crashes,
security, and the future of air safety.
    ISBN 0-7660-1108-9
    1. Aeronautics—Safety measures—Juvenile literature.
    [1. Aeronautics—Safety measures.] I. Title. II. Series: Issues
in focus (Springfield, N.J.)
    TL553.5.G26 1999
    363.12'4—DC21   98-11723
                                     CIP
                                     AC

Printed in the United States of America

10 9 8 7 6 5 4 3 2 1

To Our Readers:
All Internet addresses in this book were active and appropriate when we
went to press. Any comments or suggestions can be sent by e-mail to
Comments @enslow. com or to the address on the back cover.

Illustration Credits: Reprinted with permission of AlliedSignal
Inc. All Rights Reserved., pp. 50, 52, 64; AP/Wide World
Photos, pp. 87, 93; Boeing Commercial Airplane Group, pp. 11,
25, 41, 44, 111; Denver International Airport, p. 67; Federal
Aviation Administration, p. 33; Photo courtesy of InVision
Technologies, p. 103; Iowa State University/Center for
Nondestructive Evaluation, p. 80; Los Angeles Department of
Airports, pp. 17, 29; NASA Langley, pp. 59, 108; National
Aeronautics and Space Administration, pp. 71, 72, 75; Philip
Moylan, p. 38; Photo courtesy of Northrop Grumman
Corporation, p. 56.

Cover Illustration: Boeing Commercial Airline Group.

Contents

1

Disaster!

Everything seemed fine on the evening of July 17, 1996, when Trans World Airlines (TWA) Flight 800 took off from New York's John F. Kennedy International Airport. The weather was good, and the airplane was one of the world's mightiest jetliners—a Boeing 747. On the ground, air traffic controllers seated at radar screens tracked TWA 800 and other airplanes to ensure they all kept a safe distance from one another. The flight's 18 crew members and 212 passengers expected a peaceful flight that night across the Atlantic Ocean to Paris.

The disaster came without warning.

An Eastwind Airlines pilot saw it first: a bright light ahead of him that suddenly exploded into two fireballs. The fireballs plunged nearly three miles to the ocean below, still burning as they hit the water.[1]

The pilot radioed the air traffic controller in charge of his area. "We just saw an explosion out here," he said.

The controller, busy with another airplane, did not catch the report. "I'm sorry, I missed it."

The Eastwind pilot radioed again. "We just saw an explosion up ahead of us here . . . about 16,000 feet or something like that. It just went down—in the water."

Other pilots quickly confirmed seeing an explosion and burning debris on the water. Along the coast and on ships, hundreds of people saw a streak of light and a flash in the sky.

At the same time, TWA 800 disappeared from radar.

Between instructions to other airliners, the controller tried to contact TWA 800. "TWA 800, center," he called repeatedly. ("Center" is radio shorthand for the air traffic control center.) The airliner didn't answer.

The controller tried one more time. "TWA 800, center."

An unidentified voice came on the radio. "I think that was him."

"I think so," the controller said.

"God bless him," the voice said.[2]

Explosion in the Sky

Without warning that summer evening, a fuel tank in the belly of TWA 800 exploded. The plane's nose section tore off and tumbled away. Trailing fire and smoke, the stricken jet rolled onto its back and plunged into the ocean.[3]

Debris rained down and sank two miles to the Atlantic Ocean. All 230 people aboard the jet died.

Within hours, a massive investigation was under way to find out what had caused the crash. Two agencies led the efforts. One was the National Transportation Safety Board (NTSB), a federal agency that investigates every fatal aircraft accident in the United States. The other was the Federal Bureau of Investigation (FBI), which investigates crimes. The sudden explosion raised the question of whether a bomb had been planted on the plane, and some people who saw the streak of fire through the sky believed they had witnessed a missile attack.

Over the next seventeen months, the investigation of TWA Flight 800 would become the costliest and most extensive in aviation history. The federal government would spend more than $30 million on the probe. Divers would retrieve the remains of all the victims and more than 95 percent of the four hundred thousand pound airplane. Working in a cavernous hangar, investigators would sort through thousands of pieces of wreckage to reconstruct a ninety-four-foot-long section of the jetliner's body. Laboratories around the nation would test theories of what caused the explosion.

In December 1997, the NTSB held a weeklong public hearing on the crash in Baltimore, Maryland. Investigators said the explosion was caused by something in or near the center wing tank that ignited fuel vapors. Mixed with air, the vapors exploded with great force. The FBI had ruled out a bomb or a missile as possible causes.

Without knowing exactly what caused the explosion, the safety board left the case open.

But NTSB chairman Jim Hall said the TWA investigation had already raised several safety concerns. Most important, the research on fuel vapor had turned up new information. Researchers learned that "dangerous conditions in fuel tanks occur more commonly than has been believed."[4]

Experts said the risk of fuel tank explosions could be reduced by using fuel that produced less vapor or by filling the empty spaces in fuel tanks with a nonburning foam or nitrogen gas—something the military does with its airplanes.

At the same time, the Federal Aviation Administration (FAA) and the Boeing Company, maker of the 747, took steps to correct electrical wiring problems, acting on the possibility that worn wiring might have caused a spark that triggered the explosion.[5]

Air Travel Is Popular

Air safety is an important issue because millions of people travel by air every day. Worldwide, airlines carried almost 1.5 billion people in 1997.[6] The attention paid to safety has made flying one of the safest and most trusted forms of transportation. The crash of TWA 800 did not make people afraid to fly. NTSB chairman Jim Hall said the Boeing 747 had "registered an admirable safety record" in more than 52 million flying hours worldwide over the previous thirty years. "Whatever caused the crash of Flight 800, the explosion of a center wing tank in any aircraft is an extremely rare event," he said.[7]

Considering the number of flights made every year, airliner accidents from any cause are rare. In the United States, airliners logged 9.5 million scheduled flights in 1997, with forty-two accidents and two passenger deaths.[8]

For passengers boarding U.S. airliners that year, the odds of getting killed on a scheduled flight were less than one in 300 million.[9]

The Boeing 747 is one of the most reliable aircraft in use.

The global air safety picture is less clear, but the International Civil Aviation Organization (ICAO) reported 916 passenger deaths in twenty-six accidents involving scheduled airline flights around the world. The figures are reported by the aviation agencies of 185 nations that are members of ICAO.

In fact, air travel in 1997 caused far fewer deaths in the United States than any other form of transportation, according to NTSB figures. The safety board said highway accidents caused 42,000 deaths that year, more than 94 percent of the total (44,603) accidental deaths.

Nearly 100 died in recreational boating accidents, it said.[10]

The rarity of airliner accidents is one reason that a crash makes headlines—it is an unusual event. But a single airline crash can kill hundreds of people, making it a true disaster. Compare 1997 with the year before: In 1996, just two United States crashes claimed 340 lives—the 230 on TWA 800 and 110 who died when a ValuJet Airlines Douglas DC-9 crashed in May. Those two crashes accounted for nearly all the 380 deaths involving United States airlines that year.[11]

Crashes Shock Public

Two is a small number. But the two crashes in 1996 shocked the flying public. Each crash caused an outcry for a different reason: As difficult as it was to find out what caused TWA 800 to crash, the cause of

ValuJet Flight 592's crash was all too obvious—and preventable.

ValuJet was a fast-growing "discount" airline. Its specialty was low-cost flights between major cities. ValuJet 592 took off from Miami International Airport in Florida on May 11, 1996, with two pilots, three flight attendants, and 105 passengers on board. It was headed for Atlanta.

Nobody on board the DC-9 knew that a cargo hold in its belly contained more than one hundred canisters known as chemical oxygen generators. Chemical oxygen generators are used in some airliners as emergency oxygen sources. When activated, chemicals inside the canisters react to produce oxygen. But the reactions also generate tremendous heat. The FAA believes chemical oxygen generators are safe in airplanes if they are installed properly and maintained on a regular schedule. But they are not considered safe if they are packed into a cargo hold. The canisters in ValuJet 592's cargo hold were not supposed to be there. They also lacked required safety caps. Crash investigators believe they activated while cargo was being loaded, while the plane was taxiing, or as it took off. The result was an intense fire in the cargo hold.[12]

Six minutes into the flight, the captain and her copilot noticed electrical problems in the cockpit. The problems rapidly grew worse.

"We're losing everything," the captain said. She radioed the control tower: "We need . . . we need to go back to Miami."[13]

Behind her, the fire was burning through the floor

of the passenger cabin. Smoke was pouring in. A tape recording of the cockpit voices also picked up frantic voices from the cabin. "Fire, fire, fire, fire," a female voice said. A male voice echoed, "We're on fire. We're on fire."

While the tower radioed directions back to the airport, people in the smoke-filled cabin shouted frantically. "We need oxygen. We can't get oxygen back there," a flight attendant said.

The tower continued trying to direct the jet back toward the airport. It isn't clear whether the crew could still hear the tower or even control the airplane. It was turning back toward the airport, but suddenly the turn tightened and the plane went into a steep dive. It plunged more than a mile toward the Everglades below. It leveled out for a moment, then nosed over and slammed into the swamp. All aboard died.[14]

Although the water was only a few feet deep, the DC-9 buried itself in the oozy muck beneath the surface. Crash investigators braved alligators and snakes to recover debris, and then they spread it out in a hangar. There they found the clues to the fire that had brought down the airliner.

Chain of Errors

How had those oxygen generators ended up in the cargo hold? Why were the safety caps missing? As investigators pieced together the events leading up to the flight, they found something even more disturbing—what really caused the crash was a "chain of errors"[15] by several parties involved in the flight. Those parties were ValuJet; SabreTech, the company ValuJet hired to work on its planes; and the FAA. The safety board found that SabreTech had failed to follow proper safety practices with the canisters, marking them "empty" and allowing them to be loaded in the plane. It faulted ValuJet for failing to keep a close eye on its contractor. And it found that the FAA had ignored warnings from its own inspectors that ValuJet was not paying enough attention to safety.

One of the safety board's most alarming conclusions was that Flight 592 would likely not have crashed had the FAA required airlines to install smoke detection and fire suppression systems in airliner cargo holds—something the NTSB had recommended after another fire eight years earlier.[16] The FAA had rejected the NTSB's recommendation because its analysis concluded that the systems would not add enough safety to justify their high cost.[17]

The findings prompted strong public criticism of the government and the airline industry. Not surprisingly, the harshest words came from family members of the flight's victims. "ValuJet Flight 592 fell out of the sky because of a complete breakdown of the [safety] system," said Marilyn Chamberlin, the captain's mother.[18]

Air Safety Agencies

Two federal agencies are mainly responsible for air safety. One is the Federal Aviation Administration. It is a part of the U.S. Department of Transportation.

The FAA's responsibilities are wide ranging. It makes and enforces the rules for all aspects of civilian aviation, from manufacturing airplanes to testing pilots. FAA air traffic controllers, working in airport control towers and radar rooms, handle more than two hundred thousand takeoffs and landings every day at airports across the nation. FAA inspectors make 300,000 safety inspections of airlines and aviation activities in a year's time. FAA security people perform 30,000 security inspections and assessments, and other specialists host more than 5,000 safety seminars every year. The FAA also works with other government agencies, universities, and the aviation industry to study safety issues and develop new ways to improve safety, including new technology and new training methods.[19]

But it is also the FAA's job to assist and promote air transportation. As a result, its safety actions require a balancing act between making sure air travel is safe and ensuring that safety requirements it imposes on airline companies are not prohibitively costly.

Investigating accidents is the job of the National Transportation Safety Board. The NTSB leads the investigation of all aviation accidents and all major accidents in surface transportation, including water, highway, railroad, and pipeline. NTSB investigators are trained experts in specific areas that might be factors in a crash—engines, structures, air traffic control, or weather, to name just a few examples.

The NTSB follows what it calls a "team concept" in investigations. It includes representatives of the

Federal Aviation Administration air traffic controllers use radar and other equipment to safely guide planes while taking off, landing, and taxiing.

FAA, the airlines, airplane manufacturers, or others who might bring information or skills to an investigation. It is up to the safety board to make the final ruling on the probable cause of a crash.[20]

If the board believes the investigation has uncovered problems, it will recommend corrections. Since it was established in 1967, the board has made more than 10,700 recommendations, of which more than 3,900 were directed at aviation.[21]

The NTSB is an independent federal agency. This allows it to make recommendations that might not be popular with transportation companies or other federal agencies. It has no power to enforce its recommendations, but it has an impressive success rate—more than 82 percent of its recommendations have been accepted.[22]

The efforts of these government agencies and the aviation industry have resulted in the nation's low aircraft accident rate. It is work most air travelers take for granted and news media give little notice. As NTSB chairman Jim Hall said in 1998, "That's just the way the world works—none of us gets credit for the accident that did not occur."[23]

The Public's Role

Their two different missions sometimes put the NTSB and the FAA at odds over safety. The result can be a very highly publicized debate over air safety. This is not an accident, according to NTSB chairman Hall: "The public give-and-take of ideas on how best to assure the safety of the traveling public has been purposefully built into the system."[24]

In fact, the public is a key player in making changes in air safety, along with Congress and the news media. Said Hall:

> It would be naive to think that the public does not play a significant role in the success of our recommendation program. Often as the result of media scrutiny, public pressure is brought to bear on the recommendation recipient. If the recipient is unable to move quickly because of institutional roadblocks, the Congress often responds to lift those roadblocks—making way for the needed changes.[25]

Tragedy Spurs Action

Unfortunately, it often takes a terrible crash to focus the public's attention on a problem. An example of this was the issue of smoke detection and fire suppression systems in airliner cargo holds. The crash of ValuJet 592 made headlines nationwide. Congress, which sets the FAA's budget and oversees its operations, held hearings on the crash. Members of the public demanded changes.

The family members of ValuJet 592's victims formed an association to press for changes, something that has been done after other airline crashes. Lee Hamilton Sawyer, whose parents both died in the crash, spoke for the group at a congressional hearing. Urging Congress to force the FAA to make safety changes, Sawyer blamed their deaths on the FAA's method of weighing safety benefits against costs. "Our loved ones were sacrificed using the cost benefit analysis," she said.[26]

Changes did happen. The agency stepped up its inspection and enforcement efforts. In February 1998, it announced a new rule requiring fire detection and suppression systems in aircraft cargo holds. Complying with the new rule would not be cheap for airlines. The FAA estimated it would cost ninety thousand dollars to install the systems in each airplane already in service. And the order would require them for nearly thirty-seven hundred existing airplanes. All new airliners would also have to have them.

Investigators were still probing the ValuJet crash

when TWA 800 blew up. Although speculation about bombs and missiles would turn out to be wrong, the accident spotlighted security as a safety concern. In August 1996, President Clinton ordered a special commission to review aviation safety issues. He put Vice-President Al Gore in charge of it.

Growth Raises the Stakes

The White House Commission on Aviation Safety and Security—called the Gore Commission for short—did not find that flying was getting less safe. But it was not happy with what it did find. The accident rate for commercial aviation "declined dramatically between 1950 and 1970" to a very low level, the commission reported in February 1997. But the rate had remained "flat," getting no lower, over the past two decades.[27]

This does not bode well for the future, because more planes and people are flying every year. The FAA predicts that more than 800 million passengers will fly in the United States in the year 2007—three times the number who flew in 1980.[28]

So, even if the rate of fatal crashes stays the same, the number of fatal crashes would grow. "That's something that no one can tolerate," Gore told aviation leaders at a 1997 safety conference.[29]

One of the Gore Commission's top recommendations was for safety efforts to focus on reducing the accident rate "by a factor of five within a decade."[30]

To meet that goal, the commission urged more research, higher safety standards, better air traffic control systems, and tighter security against a growing threat of terrorist attacks.

Making an already low accident rate lower isn't easy. The Gore Commission took some criticism for not showing more clearly just how to accomplish— and pay for—the things it recommended. An editorial in *Aviation Week and Space Technology*, a respected aviation-industry journal, even warned that some of the recommendations could backfire. For example, it said that if tighter security caused too much delay and inconvenience, "many passengers will switch to riskier modes of transportation such as automobile travel, and the net effect could be more, not fewer, fatalities."[31]

No Perfect Safety

Short of grounding all airplanes, air travel can never be perfectly safe. There are many causes of airline accidents, and most accidents are caused by a combination of factors. What factors cause the most crashes, and what are the best ways to deal with them? How much are people willing to spend, either in higher taxes or more expensive airline tickets, for safer air travel? How much convenience, privacy, and freedom are they willing to sacrifice for better security?

2

From Gliders to Gridlock

The summer of 1901 did not go well for the Wright brothers. They were testing their latest design for a flying machine on the sands of Kitty Hawk, North Carolina. It was a glider. But the glider was mysteriously unstable. It kept crashing. How could they hope to fly if they could not control their flying machine? Riding a train home to Dayton, Ohio, Wilbur Wright recalled later, "I made the prediction that men would sometime fly, but that it would not be within our lifetime."[1]

Their discouragement did not last long. Back in their bicycle shop, the

Wrights started testing new ideas. In 1902, they built another glider. This one they could control. They made hundreds of long flights off a high sand dune. In 1903, they built a new machine with a gasoline engine, and on December 17 they made four powered flights. "Success," Orville Wright declared in a telegram to their family.[2] Hardly more than two years after Wilbur Wright's pessimistic prediction, the Wrights had opened the air age.

The year 2003 will mark one hundred years of powered flight—a single century in which people turned the age-old dream of wings into a global transportation system. The challenge of the next century will be to keep air travel safe as it continues to grow.

How Airplanes Fly

What the Wrights created was not just a flying machine but also a set of ideas about how to control a machine in flight—how to make it climb and turn and descend. Today, the biggest airliners and the fastest fighters reflect those basic ideas.

Flight involves the use of four forces: gravity, lift, thrust, and drag.

The first force, gravity, is what holds us to the earth. To overcome gravity, an airplane uses wings to create the second force, lift. An airplane's wings do not flap, so how do they make lift? The secret is in the wing's shape. The top surface has more curve than the bottom. As the wing moves through the air, it forces air to move over or under the wing. The curved top makes the air flowing over the wing go faster. As the air moves faster, its pressure decreases. The difference in air pressure between the bottom and the top of the wing lifts the wing upward.

Here is a simple experiment to see how lift works. Hold the end of a sheet of paper in your fingertips so that it droops. Place the end you are holding just below your lips and blow across it. The paper rises. This happens because the pressure of the air blowing over it is lower than that under it. The pressure difference is enough to lift the paper despite gravity.

The wing cannot create lift unless air is moving across it. An airplane makes this happen by moving forward through the air. What makes it move forward is the third force, thrust. This is supplied by the engine. As the engine propels the airplane faster through the air, the lifting force on the wing increases.

The fourth force is drag. This is the resistance of the air to an object moving through it. Drag works against thrust. As an airplane's speed increases, so does the drag, which is why fast planes need much more powerful engines than slow ones.

For an airplane to accelerate or climb, it must produce more thrust than the drag acting against it. And it must accelerate until the lifting force on its wing exceeds the force of gravity. When an airplane is cruising, the forces of thrust and drag balance each other, and so do lift and gravity.[3]

Airplane Controls

It took the Wright brothers years of hard work to figure out how to make a flying machine behave in the air, but today it seems downright simple. All airplanes use the same basic controls.

They include a rudder, elevators, ailerons, and flaps. Ailerons and flaps are mounted on the wings. The rudder and elevators are usually at the tail. The tail has a horizontal surface, called the horizontal stabilizer, and a vertical surface, called the vertical stabilizer.

The elevators are hinged surfaces on the back of the horizontal stabilizer. They control the airplane's up-or-down angle. The elevators are controlled by pulling or pushing on a control wheel.

To make a plane climb, you pull back on the

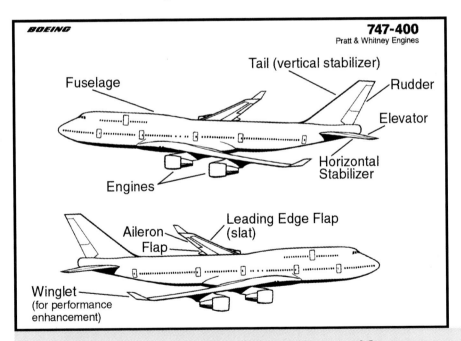

This diagram shows the rudder, elevators, ailerons, and flaps on a Boeing 747.

wheel. This tilts the elevators up. The air pushing against them pushes the tail down, which points the nose up. The opposite happens when you push the wheel forward.

The rudder is mounted on the back of the vertical stabilizer. The rudder controls the sideways, or yawing, motion of the nose. The rudder is controlled with a pair of pedals. Press on the left pedal, and the rudder will swing to the left. The air pushing on it will push the tail to the right, and the nose will yaw to the left. Press the right pedal, and the rudder will make the nose yaw to the right.

On the back of each wing is a hinged panel called an aileron. The ailerons work together to roll the airplane. Turn the wheel left, and the left aileron will go up while the right one goes down. The wind pushing on the left aileron will force the left wing down, while the wind pushing on the right one will force the right wing up.

Most airplanes also have flaps, one on the back of each wing between the fuselage and the aileron. The flaps increase the curvature of the wings. This increases lift as well as drag. Extending flaps allows a plane to fly at a slower speed and descend at a steeper angle. This allows a plane to land in a shorter distance. Many airplanes also have flaps on the front or leading edges of their wings. These are called leading-edge flaps or slats.[4]

But how the airplane reacts to these controls is not always obvious. The Wright brothers had many crashes—one hurtled Orville Wright right through a wing—before they mastered their invention.[5]

You turn a boat by turning its rudder. You can turn an airplane that way, but it does not turn very quickly. Pilots call it skidding.

The Wright brothers learned to turn an airplane by banking it. When an airplane is flying straight, its wings are lifting it vertically. But roll an airplane to make it bank, and the wings will no longer lift straight up; they will lift at the angle of bank, and the plane will try to "climb" in that direction. The result is a turn.

But that has its problems, too. The raised wing has more drag. This tends to turn the nose away from the direction of the turn. The airplane feels as if it's sliding or slipping through the turn. The rudder is used to correct the slip and produce a smooth, co-ordinated turn.

Student pilots just learning how to make turns can feel a sloppy one—it makes them slide on their seat toward the inside or outside of the turn. Now you know what it means when you hear someone talk about "flying by the seat of your pants."[6]

From Airfields to Airports

Early airplanes took off from grassy fields. The army even called its air bases "fields." But the concept changed in the early 1920s as the U.S. Post Office's airmail routes connected cities across the United States. The growing network of airfields and air routes reminded people of the long-established system of water ports and waterways.[7]

Filled with visions of commerce, cities called

their airfields airports. The desert city of Phoenix, Arizona, even has a harbor—Phoenix Sky Harbor International, its main airport.

While cities built their airports, the federal government took responsibility for the encouragement and safety of air travel. With the Air Commerce Act of 1926, Congress made the first law to standardize pilot licensing and set up a network of airways. In later years, the government would set up agencies charged with regulating the business of airlines and the safety of the sky.

Today, the Federal Aviation Administration controls most of the air space over the United States. Thousands of small airports have no control tower and are called uncontrolled airports. But most airliners use large airports that have control towers where air traffic controllers do just what their job says— they control traffic in the air. In fact, controllers also control traffic on the ground at airports. They tell airplanes when and where they may taxi, which runways to use, and when they may take off.

Air Traffic Control

Air traffic controllers use radar to track airplanes in the sky. The primary purpose of air traffic control is to keep airplanes separated to avoid collisions. To do this, the controllers talk to the pilots by radio. They advise them where nearby airplanes are and sometimes tell them to change altitude or direction.

Busy airports and fast-moving jets make air traffic control a complex operation. The control centers

Air traffic control towers are part of the network of flight service stations that provide navigation signals, flight plans, and weather information to planes.

at the busiest airports employ staffs of controllers who focus on specific parts of the job. One controller might control only airplanes on the ground. Another might handle only airplanes that are landing and taking off. Working behind radar screens, other controllers direct airplanes as they approach or leave the vicinity of the airport. Finally, special control centers called air route traffic control centers track the flow of air traffic more than ten thousand feet above sea level.

Besides controllers, the FAA has a network of flight service stations that provides weather information and flight planning services. It also maintains radio beacons that broadcast navigation signals.

It requires a lot of training for pilots and air traffic controllers to make it all work. But it does work: 625 million passengers boarded United States scheduled airlines in 1997 with only two deaths and twenty-one serious injuries. Of the preceding fifteen years, only in 1985 were the odds of dying in an airline crash more than one in a million, and then just barely so.[8]

International Cooperation

The United States is not the only country with such a complex web of air traffic control. Many parts of the airspace system have been developed through international cooperation. The International Civil Aviation Organization works to standardize the methods and rules nations use in air transportation. Standardization is important for international flights, where pilots fly out of one nation's control system and into another's.[9]

The United States has been a leader in setting international standards. Beginning with the airplane itself, much of the technology behind air safety has been developed by the United States. The United States also wields a lot of influence because of the size of its commercial aviation industry—$300 billion in 1996, according to the Gore Commission.

Modernizing the System

The biggest challenge to this web of air traffic services is the continuing growth of air traffic. New technology is needed to keep pace with the increasing numbers of planes taking off and landing at airports. By 1996, the United States was nearing the saturation point at its major airports and airways. Congress created a special commission, the National Civil Aviation Review Commission, to study the issue. Its final report in 1997 issued a serious warning. Without major changes, it said,

> our nation's aviation system will succumb to gridlock. Delays will skyrocket while we reminisce about the "reliable" flight schedules of the past. This current course will impair our domestic economy, reduce our standing in the global marketplace, and result in a long term deterioration of aviation safety.[10]

The FAA has been working on a major plan to modernize the United States air traffic control system since 1981. It holds great promise. New computers will give controllers a better picture of the air traffic flowing into and out of airports. The Global Positioning System, a constellation of navigation satellites that broadcasts radio signals, will replace less accurate ground-based beacons. The plan also envisions a more efficient routing system called "Free Flight" that would allow planes to fly more direct routes and avoid getting backed up along narrow airways.

It's a big undertaking. New equipment, from radars to computer systems, must be developed, tested, and installed. New software must be written and checked. And they must all work together, sharing vast amounts of data across nationwide networks and among thousands of air traffic controllers.

It has not gone smoothly. The modernization plan has been plagued with problems that have caused delays and higher costs. Critics have accused the FAA of mismanaging the plan, wasting billions of dollars, and losing precious time. The General Accounting Office (GAO) is an office of Congress that studies government budgets and spending. A 1996 GAO report said the FAA spent $22 billion on its modernization plan between 1981 and 1986. It also said the FAA expected to spend another $13 billion on modernization by the end of 2003. But it said the delays and costs "raise questions about the agency's ability" to meet its goals.[11]

The GAO detailed what it called "the most vivid example" of the FAA's management problems. This was the FAA's plan to replace its air traffic control computers with more modern machines and software. It said the FAA estimated the project's cost at $2.5 billion in 1983. But the FAA had to reorganize

Jane F. Garvey is the administrator of the Federal Aviation Administration and is overseeing its modernization program.

the project in 1994 after costs grew to $7.6 billion and work fell eight years behind schedule.[12]

The GAO blamed the problems on the FAA's management "culture," or the manner in which it planned and managed modernization work. It gave the agency credit for recognizing the problem and taking steps to fix it. The National Civil Aviation Review Commission also found problems in the FAA's management style, as well as in how the agency is funded. Federal laws also limited the FAA's ability to manage big modernization projects efficiently, the commission said.

FAA administrator Jane Garvey joined the FAA in 1997, after the modernization plan had been under way for years. She reorganized the program to speed up work on the least troubled parts, while pushing back the schedule on the most troubled ones. Congress debated changing laws that control the FAA's funding and its requirements for managing contracts.

The modernization plan still has years to go as this book is written, and its outcome is not clear. What is clear is that air travel has evolved from a single primitive flying machine to a complex, global operation in less than a century. Likewise, the business of air safety has become ever more complex, and it depends as much on wise public officials as on skillful pilots and controllers.

Human Error

There is an old joke that the airplane of the future will have two crew members, a pilot and a German shepherd. The pilot's job, goes the joke, will be to feed the German shepherd. The German shepherd's job will be to bite the pilot if he tries to touch the controls.

Although the military is making more use of robot spy planes, there is little talk in the airline industry about taking humans out of the cockpit. Automatic pilots often control cruising airliners, but they cannot respond to emergencies. Even when a plane is on automatic pilot, the human pilot is still in charge—still responsible for the safety of everyone aboard.

Yet, more than 70 percent of airline accidents since the 1950s have involved human error.[1] The reason is simple: While airplanes, weather reporting, and air traffic control have improved dramatically in the first century of powered flight, human behavior still has age-old imperfections.[2]

Accidents such as those described in this chapter have provided valuable information on the effects of human error and ways to prevent or guard against it. It would be better to learn about problems before accidents happen. In fact, one of the challenges to air safety is finding new ways to detect problems before they turn into accidents.

"Pilot error" is the cause given for many crashes. This is because the pilot—more specifically, the captain—is responsible for the safe operation of the airplane. But pilots are not the only ones who make errors that figure in accidents. Studies have found that most airplane crashes over the years involve errors by more than one person. Those others may include other crew members, air traffic controllers, pilots in other aircraft, maintenance workers, and even airline management.

David Beaty, a British pilot, psychologist, and author, says the term pilot error is giving way to the concept of "human error."

Over the years, safety experts have become aware that many deadly aviation errors stem from common patterns of human behavior. They are also paying more attention to how humans interact with machines, a field of study known as human factors. In his book *The Naked Pilot*, Beaty says understanding the role of human behavior in aircraft accidents is "the last great frontier in aviation."[3]

Government and industry are battling human error with technology and training. Better technology can help guard against human error. For example, new safety systems in the cockpit give better warnings when airplanes are straying into danger. Better training helps prevent human error, both in the cockpit and in air traffic control centers.

The Gore Commission spotlighted the need for more work on the human side of aviation safety. "Government and industry aviation safety research should emphasize human factors and training," it said in its 1997 report to President Clinton.[4]

Errors Cost Lives

Human error was responsible for the worst commercial air disaster as of this writing. On March 27, 1977, two Boeing 747s collided on a fog-shrouded runway on Tenerife, one of the Canary Islands in the Atlantic Ocean. That crash killed 583 people.

Several factors set the stage for disaster. A terrorist bombing had closed an airport on a nearby island, forcing a number of aircraft to land at Tenerife until the other airport reopened. Among them were a KLM Royal Dutch Airlines Boeing 747 and a Pan American World Airways Boeing 747. When the other airport reopened, the airplanes were at the wrong end of the Tenerife runway for takeoff.

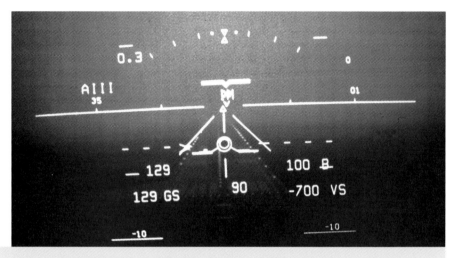

A Heads-Up Guidance System (HGS) displays critical information for a pilot landing a plane in low visibility conditions. Such high-tech equipment can help reduce pilot error in certain situations.

The taxiways were jammed, so they slowly taxied one after another down the runway.

By then, a thick fog had blanketed the airport. The KLM and Pan Am pilots could not see each other's airplanes, and air traffic controllers could not see either one. It was a confusing situation. Everybody had to rely on radios to learn where other airplanes were and when the runway was clear for takeoff.

The captain of the KLM jet faced a time crunch. Passengers were waiting at the other airport. The jet was to pick them up and complete a flight to Amsterdam. But the crew members were close to the limit of how long they were allowed to be on duty. If they did not get going soon, the whole flight might be stuck until a relief crew arrived.[5]

The KLM jet reached the end of the runway and turned around. The Pan Am jet was still creeping down the runway. Its pilots peered through the fog for a taxiway where they could turn off to make way for the KLM jet.

As soon as he heard the controller say he was "clear," the KLM captain pushed the throttles to takeoff power. His copilot quickly radioed that they were "at takeoff" or "now taking off."[6]

But the controller had cleared the jet for only its route after takeoff, not the takeoff itself. And the controller did not seem to understand that the KLM jet was actually starting its takeoff roll because he simply told the pilot to "stand by for takeoff. I will call you."[7] At the same instant, the Pan Am jet radioed that it was "still taxiing down the runway."

The two calls interfered with each other, and all the KLM crew heard was a loud squeal on their radio.

Takeoff Without Clearance

A moment later, the Pan Am crew told the tower it would "report when we're clear." The KLM flight engineer apparently heard that because he asked, "Is he not clear, that Pan American?"

But the KLM captain replied, "Oh yes."[8]

Down the runway, the Pan Am crew was still searching for its turnoff when the KLM jet hurtled into view. The Pan Am jet went to full throttle and turned to get off the runway, desperately trying to avoid the onrushing jumbo jet. The Pan Am copilot shouted, "Get off! Get off! Get off!"[9]

The KLM crew got its huge, heavy jet airborne, but the main landing gear smashed into the Pan Am's fuselage. The damaged KLM 747 dropped back onto the runway and erupted in flames. All of the jet's 248 occupants died in the fire.

The collision ripped open the Pan Am jet and set it afire. Emergency exits were destroyed. Passengers and crew members had to jump through holes high on the side of the 747. Only 59 of the 394 people on the Pan Am plane survived.

Since the Canary Islands are Spanish, Spain led the crash investigation. United States and Dutch authorities were permitted to participate. The Spanish investigation board found the KLM pilot at fault for starting his takeoff without being cleared to do so. But the investigation found that human factors contributed to the disaster in several ways.

One was the confusion in communications. The KLM copilot and controllers spoke to each other in English, the standard language for international flights. But they did not use the precise words or phrases that are called for in aviation communications. The captain did not wait for the specific instruction clearing him for takeoff. Likewise, the copilot did not use the correct words when he told the controllers that the jet was starting its takeoff roll.

Copilot Did Not Question Captain

Spanish and United States investigators believed another factor in the crash was the reluctance of the KLM's copilot to challenge his captain's actions. The

KLM captain was one of the airline's most senior pilots and an experienced flight instructor. KLM even used his picture in advertisements. The investigators suggested that the KLM copilot, younger and far less experienced, viewed his captain as an authority not to be questioned. Dutch investigators disagreed.

This crash and others in the 1970s reinforced studies that found human error at work in most fatal plane crashes. Together, they focused attention on the need for teamwork in the cockpit. This concept is now commonly known as crew resource management. It holds that crew performance is

Communication in the cockpit is the most effective way to prevent accidents.

better when crew members coordinate their activities and question one another's actions. United Airlines pioneered the development of formal crew resource management training programs, and the concept gradually gained acceptance throughout the industry. In 1996, the FAA issued a rule that would require airline crew members to have this training by March 1998.[10] The International Civil Aviation Organization also requires it for airlines that make international flights.[11]

Teamwork Saves Lives

In contrast to the deadly errors that led to the Tenerife crash, crew teamwork saved 184 lives in a United Airlines accident on July 19, 1989.

United Flight 232 was a McDonnell Douglas DC-10. It was bound from Denver to Chicago when one of its engines blew up. Jet engines have large fans inside them that spin at high speed to compress air before it is mixed with fuel and burned. The DC-10 has three engines, one under each wing and one in the tail. A big, rapidly rotating fan disk in the rear engine of Flight 232 broke, shooting pieces through the tail of the plane and cutting its control lines. The copilot reported he could not control the plane as it started veering to the right. The captain was able to straighten out the plane by reducing thrust in the left engine. The crew requested an emergency landing at Sioux Gateway Airport in Sioux City, Iowa, and told the chief flight attendant to prepare the plane's 285 passengers for an emergency landing.

A flight attendant told them an off-duty United DC-10 pilot was among the passengers. They asked him to join them in the cockpit. "We don't have any controls," the captain told him. Without flight controls, the situation looked hopeless. The captain told his crew, "We're not gonna make the runway, fellas."[12]

But they did not give up. The regular crew and the off-duty pilot worked as a team to do something nobody had ever tried: steer a DC-10 by adjusting power on its two wing-mounted engines. While the regular crew members dumped fuel, put down the landing gear, and talked to air traffic controllers, the off-duty pilot worked the throttles with both hands. He was trying to steer the plane on a gently descending path toward the airport. But it was hard to keep the wings level, and they could not stop the nose from bobbing slowly up and down. Through it all, crew members continually shared information and suggestions.[13]

Soon the airport was in sight. The crew lined the plane up on a runway. The flaps did not work, so they could not use them to slow down. They could not cut the engines because they needed them to steer the airplane. They came in at almost 250 miles per hour, much faster than normal. They were close to touchdown when the nose dipped again. The right wing scraped the ground. The giant jet cartwheeled across the runway and caught fire, then slammed onto its back. The crash killed 111 passengers and one flight attendant. But the actions of the three crew

A flight simulator allows pilots to train for difficult flying conditions without risk to lives and airplanes.

members, the off-duty pilot, and the flight attendants saved 184 others.

The NTSB reenacted the emergency, using a DC-10 flight simulator. In the tests, pilots found it "virtually impossible" to make a controlled landing without the use of flight controls. Instead of finding any faults in the United Flight 232 crew's actions, the simulations showed how well they had done against overwhelming odds. The safety board found the crew's performance was highly commendable and greatly exceeded reasonable expectations.[14]

Worst Killer: Flying into Ground

Weather, in the form of fog, was a factor in the crash on Tenerife Island. Mechanical failure in an engine caused the crash of United Flight 232 at Sioux City. But air safety experts say most fatal accidents are caused when properly working airplanes are simply flown into the ground. These are called controlled-flight-into-terrain (CFIT) accidents. Government and industry safety authorities say CFIT accidents cause more than half of all airline deaths worldwide. In 1997, Stuart Matthews, chairman, president, and chief executive officer of the nonprofit Flight Safety Foundation, called CFIT accidents "the number one killer of passengers and crew aboard commercial transport aircraft."[15]

CFIT accidents are not new. United States airliners were flying into the ground from one to four times per year from the mid-1960s through the early

1970s,[16] until a series of terrible crashes focused attention on the problem.

On December 12, 1972, Eastern Airlines Flight 401 was bound for Miami, Florida, from John F. Kennedy International Airport in New York. When the crew lowered the landing gear of the Lockheed L-1011, a green light did not come on to indicate the nose gear was down and locked in place.

The pilots set the autopilot for two thousand feet and let the plane circle while they tried to figure out whether the problem was with the landing gear or the light. They did not notice the autopilot turn off—something that should have been monitored—or the chime that sounded when the plane started a gentle descent. The view out the window, in the moonless night sky over the Everglades, showed only darkness.

An air traffic controller noticed the altitude change but did not question it when he radioed, "How are things coming along out there?"[17]

The pilots noticed their altitude too late. The big jet hit the swamp and disintegrated. The crash killed five crew members and ninety-six passengers. An investigation showed the nosegear was fine; the little green light had burned out.

Just two years later, on December 1, 1974, another headline-making crash spurred the FAA to action. TWA Flight 514, a Boeing 727 carrying ninety-two people, hit a low mountain in Virginia as it was approaching Dulles International Airport near Washington, D.C. Flying in clouds, the pilots did not see the mountain. All aboard died.

Ground Warning System

After that crash, the FAA required United States scheduled airlines to carry a special device called a ground proximity warning system (GPWS) that would alert crews when the plane was getting too close to the ground. The rate of controlled-flight-into-terrain accidents dropped dramatically.

GPWS could provide warnings against many dangerous situations. It bounced a radio signal off the ground below the airplane to keep track of its altitude, and it used data from other equipment to tell whether the airplane was doing something unusual and possibly dangerous. It could sound a warning if an airplane was banking too steeply at a low altitude, descending too quickly, or simply getting too close to the ground.

But the system was not foolproof. For one thing, it could not guard against what pilots called the "vertical cliff" problem—sharply rising peaks or ridges ahead of the airplane. Also, the system would not signal alerts if an airplane was on a steady descent path with its landing gear and flaps down, as on a routine landing approach.[18]

Night Flight in Mountains

American Airlines Flight 965, a Boeing 757, was on an evening flight from Miami to Alfonso Bonilla Aragon International Airport in Cali, Colombia, on December 20, 1995. The airport was located in a long valley that ran north to south. Its elevation was about three thousand feet above sea level. On either side, the landscape wrinkled up into high mountain ridges with peaks reaching 14,000 feet.

When the crew radioed the airport, a controller cleared them for a straight-in approach that would involve homing on a radio beacon near the runway. The pilots programmed a new flight plan into the airplane's flight management computer. But they punched in a single-letter code that identified the wrong radio beacon. This simple error aimed the plane not at the beacon near the airport but a different one 150 miles to the east, in the midst of high mountains. It was the first in a fatal chain of errors.[19]

Busy checking charts and controls, the pilots apparently did not notice as the plane made a turn to the east. More than a minute later the copilot said, "Where are we?"

They became confused about their course. But instead of catching their error, they tried to make sense of a flight plan they thought must be correct. The copilot asked whether they should turn around. "Nawww . . . let's press on to . . ." said the captain. The copilot said, "Well, we're . . . press on to where, though?"[20]

They requested a change in directions from the controller. The request did not make sense to the controller, who expected the airplane to be heading straight for the airport. He had no way of checking the plane's course because the airport had no radar. But the controller did not speak English well enough to question them. (Although pilots and controllers are required to communicate in English on international flights, the controller spoke mainly Spanish, Colombia's national language.)

In the darkness, Flight 965 wandered into a valley edged with high ridges. By now it was below 9,000 feet. Suddenly, the GPWS began whooping an alarm. "Terrain, terrain," a mechanical voice warned. The crew pushed the throttles to full power and tried to climb. "Pull up, baby," the captain said. But there was not enough time. The jet cut through the trees as it climbed the ridge, then crashed to the ground on the other side. A search helicopter found the wreckage the next day. Only four out of 163 people on board survived the crash.[21]

Improving Technology

Colombian authorities listed several causes for the accident, all of them dealing with the crew's actions. They especially noted the crew's all-too-human reluctance to change a decision—in this case, to abandon a flight plan that had become confusing.

Despite the pilots' mistakes, an earlier warning about the ridge might have prevented the crash. Such a system had just been developed. It was called an Enhanced Ground Proximity Warning System (EGPWS). It combined navigation data with an electronic map of the world. Anywhere an airplane flew with EGPWS, a screen in the cockpit could display a view of the ground around the airplane. It would signal a warning about dangerous ground ahead.

In the wake of the Cali crash, the National Transportation Safety Board made several

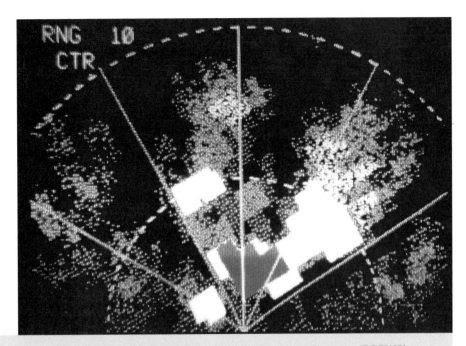

The Enhanced Ground Proximity Warning System (EGPWS) combines navigation data with electronic maps to prevent controlled flight into terrain accidents. The dark gray area inside the inner circle indicates high terrain.

recommendations to the FAA. One was to study EGPWS technology to see if it could be effective in cases where GPWS was not. The FAA concluded that EGPWS would prevent more accidents than GPWS. In August 1998, the FAA proposed a rule that would require EGPWS systems on all jets or turbine-powered propeller planes with six or more passenger seats.[22]

Safety Technology Is Costly

Using technology to guard against human errors is not cheap. The FAA estimated the new rule would affect more than seven thousand airplanes and cost the airline industry more than $400 million. But it also estimated that, by reducing the number of crashes, the new systems would save the industry more than $5 billion in the long run.[23]

Most major airlines had already decided to adopt the new technology. When the FAA approved the new systems for use in 1996, well before proposing the rule to require it, American Airlines made a $20 million order to equip its fleet of 635 aircraft by mid-1999.[24]

In December 1997, the Air Transport Association (ATA) announced a voluntary program in which its members would install EGPWS in their aircraft. ATA is a trade organization whose member airlines carry nearly all of the United States's air passengers and freight. The program would put EGPWS in about forty-three hundred airplanes. "Accidents in which aircraft run into the ground or mountains are the number-one global aviation safety problem. Installation of this new safety system will largely eliminate this type of accident," ATA President Carol Hallett said.[25]

Learning from Incidents

Accidents such as those described in this chapter offer valuable lessons in air safety. Obviously, it would be better to learn these lessons before an accident happens. And this will have to happen if the accident rate is to be pushed lower than it already is. One way to do this is to learn from incidents—

Called "black boxes," flight recorders record all cockpit communications as well as crucial flight data, including altitude, direction, airplane performance, and weather conditions.

situations in which problems occur but do not result in accidents.

One key to this approach already exists. The flight data recorders airliners carry do not just record data during a crash. Throughout the flight, they record what is happening to the engines, the flight controls, and many other parts of the plane. Safety analysts can use the data to spot problems with the plane or potentially dangerous practices by the crew. These problems can then be corrected, possibly preventing an accident down the road.

Several airlines routinely analyze the data from

their flight recorders. The FAA and industry leaders agree that it would be better to share the results so that everyone could learn from one another's experiences. They even have a name for the concept: Flight Operations and Quality Assurance.

What has held up use of this concept is the fear among airlines and pilots that the FAA will take action against them if the data show they accidentally violated aviation rules. Safety experts believe many problems go unreported now because of this fear.

It is a concern the FAA itself has acknowledged. A new strategic plan it released in 1998 stated, "[The] FAA must balance its enforcement activities with the need to share information in order to garner the maximum improvement in safety."[26]

Airlines and individuals want guarantees that the information they share will not be used against them by the FAA, turned over to the news media for sensational stories, or used as evidence against them in lawsuits. But this would require new aviation rules or even changes in federal laws, and in late 1998 the aviation industry was still waiting.

4

Weather

One reason that air travel is popular is because it saves time. Instead of spending days on a bus or a train, one can jet across the United States in just a few hours. Air travel allows people to reach almost any point on earth within a few days. Time is important to most air travelers, especially people traveling on business. They want to know when their flights will leave and arrive. Airlines that want to stay in business must have schedules and stick to them.

This means airplanes must be able to fly safely by day and at night, in good weather and bad. The FAA, National Weather Service, and Department of Defense weather services work together to provide aviation weather information. Weather information is available to pilots when they plan flights or as they are flying. Pilots themselves are a part of the weather information system—the FAA encourages them to radio pilot reports (called pireps) as they fly. Pilots also rely on a wide variety of weather and navigation aids, from cockpit instruments that help them fly in clouds to radio beacons, radar, and weather satellites. Pressurized planes fly above the clouds, where the air is usually smooth and passengers can enjoy a comfortable ride.

Most accidents are caused by human error, but weather is still a challenge to air safety. The earth's weather system is extremely complex. It continues to surprise scientists who study it, not to mention pilots who fly in it.

It is important to develop technologies that can predict dangerous weather and get the information to pilots. This involves important decisions about which technologies to spend money on and how quickly to put new systems into operation. It is also important to make sure that airplanes are properly equipped for the weather they fly in and that crews are trained in the correct procedures for dangerous weather.

Early Airlines and Weather

Flying was an adventure in the early days of airline travel. Navigation aids were primitive. Weather

Radar is used to track aircraft and detect dangerous weather. This ASR-9 airport surveillance radar tracks aircraft in the vicinity of an airport.

reporting was spotty. Pilots relied on their knowledge of landmarks for navigation and their steel-nerved flying skills for dealing with weather. They plowed through snow, rain, and thunderstorms, bucking the wild winds like rodeo riders.

In the 1920s, the government set up flashing beacons to mark airways across the United States. But the beacons worked only as long as pilots could see them. Clouds or fog could hide them. The answer was a beacon that could pierce the clouds—a radio beacon. In 1929, air pioneer (and, later, World War II hero) Jimmy Doolittle demonstrated the first "blind" takeoff, flight, and landing, using only radio aids for navigation.

Doolittle also used new instruments that told him his airplane's attitude—how its wings were banked and how its nose was pitched. These instruments were critical to flying in clouds or at night, when there was no visible horizon to help a pilot know which way was up.

Radio navigation could help an airplane find its way through clouds. But the clouds themselves could harbor dangers visible only as ominous darkenings in the cloud or as sudden flashes of light—thunderstorms.

Flying Above Storms

Thunderstorms are violent things. They generate strong winds, hail, and lightning. The edge of a weather system, called a front, can throw up a wall of thunderstorms to block an airplane's path. In hot weather, individual thunderstorms can boil up quickly.

One solution is to avoid clouds by flying above them. In the 1930s, the Army and the airlines began making experimental flights into the stratosphere— high altitudes (from seven to thirty miles above earth) where the air is smooth—above the rough-and-tumble weather of clouds and storms. But the air gets thinner with altitude, which means there is less oxygen to breathe. At around 30,000 feet or higher, people quickly become unconscious without extra oxygen.[1]

Aviation pioneer Wiley Post made high-altitude flights in 1931 with a suit and helmet that surrounded his body with pressurized air. It was the earliest forerunner of the space suit. But it would hardly be practical for planeloads of passengers to bundle up in bulky pressure suits. The solution was to pressurize the whole cabin. In 1940, Boeing produced the 307 Stratoliner, the world's first pressurized airliner.

Wind Shear

But airplanes must still grapple with weather at airports. And we are still learning about weather—sometimes the hard way.

Until the 1970s, weather researchers believed the main threat to airplanes taking off or landing in thunderstorms was a sudden change in wind speed and direction ahead of a storm. Such a sudden change is known as a wind shear.

A wind shear changes an airplane's speed relative to the air around it. Imagine an airplane is flying over the ground at one hundred miles per hour while flying directly into a ten-mile-per-hour wind. The plane's speed through the air is actually 110 miles per hour. This is called its airspeed. Now, imagine the wind suddenly reverses direction, from a ten-mile-per-hour head wind to a ten-mile-per-hour tailwind. The plane's airspeed is suddenly reduced by twenty

A downdraft over a runway threatens an approaching airliner in this NASA illustration. The wind is blowing downward from the bottom of a thunderstorm, then fanning out in all directions. Unlike the illustration, downdrafts cannot be seen, but wind sensors and radar can detect them.

miles per hour. A sudden loss of airspeed reduces the amount of lift an airplane's wings create, and it can cause an airplane to start dropping. This can be dangerous if an airplane is flying low and slow, as on a landing approach.

Storms can produce wind shears in ways that are much more complex and dangerous than people imagined until the 1970s. In 1974, an unusual outbreak of severe thunderstorms left odd patterns of destruction on the ground. T. Theodore Fujita, a professor of meteorology at the University of Chicago, noticed mysterious "starburst" patterns of flattened trees and damaged property.

Microbursts

These were the telltale signs of what Fujita later named microbursts. A microburst is a compact, powerful downdraft that starts high in the air and fans outward near the ground. It creates a series of dangerous wind shears. Fujita defined microbursts as being less than 2.5 miles across and lasting for only a matter of minutes.

Microbursts are most dangerous to airplanes that are flying close to the ground at low speed, typically approaching or leaving an airport. A plane that enters a microburst first gets a head wind. To maintain airspeed and rate of descent, the pilot will normally reduce power. Next comes a powerful downdraft, followed by a tailwind. The downdraft drives the plane toward the ground, and the tailwind rapidly reduces its airspeed. Already flying at reduced power, the plane may crash into the ground before the pilot can get it to climb.

Fujita was studying microburst clues when an airliner crash tragically provided fresh ones. On June 24, 1975, Eastern Airlines Flight 66, a Boeing 727, was approaching Runway 22 Left at John F. Kennedy International Airport in New York. There was a strong thunderstorm near the airport. Pilots of airplanes ahead of the Eastern flight were reporting strong wind shears.

A Flying Tiger DC-8 approaching Runway 22 Left

suddenly found itself losing airspeed and dropping. The captain pushed the engines to full power to avoid hitting the ground. When he landed, he reported "a tremendous wind shear."

He urged air traffic controllers to tell the airplanes behind him to use a different runway.[2] Just behind the DC-8, another Eastern flight broke off its approach to Runway 22 Left. The captain reported "a pretty good shear pulling us to the right and . . . down." He, too, had to pour on power to avoid hitting the ground.[3] Two other planes also reported airspeed losses and high rates of descent.

The controllers continued to direct traffic to Runway 22 Left, and Flight 66 continued its approach. Leading to the runway was a series of towers holding lights that marked the approach to the runway. As Flight 66 descended toward the runway, flight data later showed, its rate of descent suddenly doubled, and its airspeed dropped. Less than a half mile from the runway, Flight 66 struck one of the towers. The outer left wing broke off, and the plane burst into flames. The burning plane crashed through more towers before hitting the ground and skidding to a stop on a road. The crash killed 113 of the 124 people on board.

Based on cockpit conversations, investigators concluded the Flight 66 pilots were looking out the windshield for the runway instead of at their gauges, so they did not notice the changes in airspeed and altitude. But even if they had, the safety board concluded, "the adverse winds might have been too severe for a successful approach and landing."[4] A contributing factor, the board said, was the continued use of Runway 22 Left when the wind shear danger "should have become evident" to controllers and pilots alike.[5]

Wind Shear Detection Systems

The Boeing 727 jet had fallen victim to a microburst. Microbursts would continue to threaten air safety because they could go undetected by the systems being developed to warn of wind shear.

In 1976, the FAA developed the Low Level Wind Shear Alert System (LLWAS) and installed it at major airports over the next few years. An LLWAS uses several detectors located around an airport to measure differences in wind; a large difference in readings would indicate a wind shear. But the system cannot measure winds above ground level, and it is sometimes slow to trigger alerts.

The delay proved deadly on July 9, 1982. Pan Am Flight 759, a Boeing 727, encountered a wind shear that afternoon as it tried to take off from New Orleans International Airport. It started to climb, then fell back. It struck trees off the end of the runway and crashed into houses. All 145 people aboard the airplane and eight on the ground died in the crash. A National Aeronautics and Space Administration (NASA) report said the airport's LLWAS triggered an alert two seconds after the airplane hit the trees.[6]

The FAA was studying the wind shear threat and

moving toward requiring a detection system on airplanes when another microburst struck.

A thunderstorm had boiled up quickly over the approach route to Dallas/Fort Worth International Airport on August 2, 1985. Delta 191, a Lockheed L-1011, was coming in with 163 people on board. The jet ran into heavy rain, a series of updrafts and downdrafts, and a head wind that increased rapidly. Just as the copilot reduced power, the wind switched to a powerful tailwind. The jet plummeted. The co-pilot poured on power, but the airplane smashed into the ground, broke apart, and burned. Only twenty-six people survived, fifteen with serious injuries. Again, the LLWAS on the airport did not sound an alert until after the crash.[7]

The crash sparked a public outcry for protection. Congress quickly approved additional funds for a major wind shear research program. Earlier studies had already shown that some microbursts were too powerful for any airliner. The need was clear for devices that could warn pilots of microbursts before they flew into them.

Doppler Radar, Airborne Detectors

The only way to test different devices was to install them in an airplane and fly through a microburst. Researchers with NASA and the FAA outfitted a Boeing 737 for the tests. They studied special flying procedures to escape microbursts, but it was still a risky program. In 1991 and 1992, they made flight after flight through dark skies full of rain, flashing

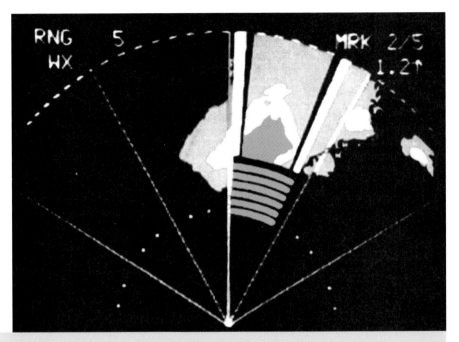

Radar on board airplanes can warn pilots before they fly into wind shears. The striped fan-shaped symbol just right of the center of the photograph indicates a wind shear condition.

lightning, and jolting wind shears. They found that the best technology available was a kind of radar called Doppler radar. Mounted in a plane's nose, it bounces radar waves off water droplets and other particles in the air to measure changes in wind velocities. A big change would indicate a wind shear.

Meanwhile, the FAA was developing an airport-based system called the Terminal Doppler Weather Radar. In 1991, the agency announced that Doppler radar would soon be installed at major airports where thunderstorms were a serious problem. But the program fell behind schedule because of technical problems, lack of funding, and difficulty finding good sites for the radar stations near some airports.

Charlotte/Douglas International Airport in North Carolina was one of the airports selected to receive the radar. But it was still on the waiting list when USAir Flight 1016, a DC-9, tried to land there on July 2, 1994. A thunderstorm was building between the jet and the airport, but air traffic controllers did not alert the crew to dangerous winds, a subsequent investigation found. The jet was equipped with an onboard wind shear alert system, but it also failed to alert them. The jet entered a microburst and plunged to the ground. Thirty-seven people died in the crash.

The NTSB's findings cited the crew's failure to recognize dangerous weather and take evasive action, but most of its findings dealt with the problem of getting critical weather information to the pilots.

Technology and Funding Set Pace

One problem the report noted was the FAA's delays in the Terminal Doppler Weather Radar program. Critics said the FAA should have made the program a higher priority. For example, the agency spent money to upgrade the LLWAS systems at many airports in the 1980s instead of spending more money on the radar program. The agency blamed technical problems that made it hard to develop a reliable system. For example, it said tests at different airports showed local conditions often affected what the radar showed.[8]

Congress got some blame, too, because it controls the FAA's funding. "What Congress gives this year, can be taken away or reduced next year. It makes it hard to plan, or carry out long-term projects," John Mazor, spokesman for the Air Line Pilots Association, said in the *Charlotte Observer*.[9] As of late 1998, the FAA said terminal weather radars were up and running at thirty-eight major airports out of the forty-five scheduled to get them.

The onboard wind shear alert system was also faulted. In 1990, the FAA had ordered commercial aircraft to have such systems by the end of 1993. But the systems available at that time were so-called reactive systems. They used data from the airplane's other instruments to detect when the plane was entering a wind shear. Newer systems coming along used an on-board Doppler radar to send out beams that would detect wind shear up to a minute before the airplane reached it. The first system of this type was approved for use on September 1, 1994.[10]

Pilots Need Information

Much of the problem boiled down to getting information to the pilots. The NTSB report criticized FAA policies and communication breakdowns in the Charlotte control tower that prevented the USAir Flight 1016 crew from learning about the wind shear. The National Research Council, a private, nonprofit organization, said the FAA should make it a higher priority to get weather information to pilots. "During bad weather, air traffic controllers may be so

Denver International Airport is one of the newest, largest, and most technologically up-to-date airports in the world.

busy tracking aircraft that they have little time to study weather conditions," the council said.[11]

The research council said technology already existed that could help. It pointed out an irony of modern technology: With a laptop computer, a modem, and a telephone, a passenger can tap a wealth of up-to-the-minute weather information on the Internet.

"In many cases, this information is superior to that available to pilots in the cockpit," the research council said.[12]

Work is being done to get this kind of information into the cockpit. For several years, the FAA has been developing a new system that would weave together data from weather and air traffic control radars. Computer programs would use the data to predict the movement of storms and the development of dangerous conditions several minutes before they actually arise. It would present the information to air traffic controllers in easy-to-understand graphics and text. It could also be transmitted directly to pilots in airplanes outfitted with the proper equipment. The FAA calls it the Integrated Terminal Weather System and awarded a contract to develop the system in January 1995. It said it planned to install it in thirty-four locations nationwide between the years 2000 and 2003.[13] But, like so many of the FAA's big projects, it has had cost increases and delays.[14]

Icing

Icing is another major threat to airplanes. Freezing rain and snow can form ice on airplane wings, interrupting the smooth flow of air over the wings. This robs them of lift and increases drag and weight. It doesn't take much ice to be dangerous, the FAA warns:

> Ice, snow, or frost formations having a thickness and surface roughness similar to medium or coarse sandpaper on the leading edge and upper surface of a wing can reduce wing lift by as much as 30 percent and increase drag by 40 percent.[15]

Federal aviation rules dating back to 1950 forbid pilots from taking off with ice, snow, or even frost on airplane wings. In wet, freezing weather, ground crews hose down airliners with specially formulated fluids to remove ice and temporarily prevent it from reforming. Many airplanes have heaters and other deicing and anti-ice equipment. But crashes in which ice played a role have underscored the importance of setting safe standards for flying in icy conditions. These standards range from how ice is removed from airplanes on the ground to how well their anti-ice systems must work in the air.

Icing Before Takeoff

A snowstorm in Washington, D.C., set the stage for a horrific crash on January 13, 1982. The heavy snow had closed the airport at one point. Air Florida Flight 90, a Boeing 737 with seventy-nine people on board, was nearly two hours behind schedule when ground crews hosed it down with deicing fluid. But there was a long line of other airplanes ahead of it, and Air Florida Flight 90 spent about another hour in the snow after deicing before it was cleared for takeoff.[16]

Despite the snow, the crew failed to turn on heaters to keep ice from blocking pressure probes in its two engines. The ice made the probes give false high-pressure readings, indicating more thrust than the engines were actually producing. The jet took off with the engines at 75 percent power instead of full power. The thrust gauges may have looked right, but the airspeed gauge may have revealed that they were accelerating too slowly. "God, look at that thing, that don't seem right, does it? . . . Ah, that's not right," the copilot, who was flying the plane, said. "Yes it is," the captain assured him.[17]

The jet lifted off, but it climbed sluggishly on the edge of a stall. Its nose pitched up steeply, something the 737 was known to do with ice on its wings.[18] "Forward, forward," the captain said. But with its nose pitched up, power back, and icy wings getting poor lift, the jet sank. It struck the Fourteenth Street Bridge, smashing vehicles and killing four people. Then it plunged into the Potomac River and disappeared beneath a layer of broken ice. A helicopter crew plucked four passengers and a flight attendant from the freezing water. No one else survived.

The NTSB blamed the crash on the pilots' failure to use engine anti-ice heaters, their decision to take off with snow and ice on the plane's wings, and the captain's failure to stop the takeoff when his copilot called attention to suspicious instrument readings. But the crash also underscored the importance of keeping wings free of snow or ice. The safety board concluded that the long delay between deicing and takeoff and the airplane's known tendency to pitch up with ice on its wings both contributed to the crash.

The FAA advised airlines and pilots on the importance of making sure airplane surfaces are clean before takeoff. But it did not issue new rules requiring specific ground operations to prevent icing until after another crash more than ten years later. USAir Flight 405, a Fokker 28 jet, crashed while trying to take off with icy wings from LaGuardia Airport in Flushing, New York, on March 22, 1992. Twenty-seven of the fifty-one people on board died.

The National Transportation Safety Board blamed "the failure of the airline industry and the Federal Aviation Administration" to create rules and procedures for pilots to guard against icing when their takeoffs are delayed after deicing.[19] It noted

that although the FAA had issued advisories, but not
rules, for preventing accidents after the Air Florida
crash, "as many as 10 icing-related accidents,
including USAir Flight 405, have occurred."[20]

In-Flight Icing

Icing can also collect on an airplane surface while a
plane is airborne. This is called in-flight icing. The
FAA requires that airplanes have the proper anti-
icing equipment before it will certify them to be
flown in icing conditions. But two terrible crashes in

*Researchers at NASA's Lewis Research Center use this
DeHavilland DH-6 Twin Otter aircraft to conduct in-flight icing
research for the Supercooled Large Droplet (SLD) program. The
aircraft is outfitted with instruments that will measure and
record large-droplet icing cloud characteristics, ice accretion on
wing surfaces, and resulting changes in aircraft performance
due to SLD ice accretions.*

The DeHavilland DH-6 Twin Otter aircraft is shown after flying in a supercooled large droplet condition. Ice is found covering the aircraft.

the 1990s revealed weaknesses in that process as well as in information and training for pilots.

On October 31, 1994, American Eagle Flight 4184, a French-built ATR-72, crashed after it encountered freezing drizzle in a cloud.

The ATR-72 is one of several types of small airliners known as commuters. Commuter planes are popular with airlines that fly small numbers of passengers on short routes, mainly between smaller airports and major airline hubs. They typically haul fewer than one hundred passengers—the ATR-72 seats up to seventy-four—and many use propellers instead of jets. Commuters fly lower and slower than jets, so they are more likely to fly in clouds that can contain icing conditions.

American Eagle Flight 4184 was circling in a holding pattern over Chicago's O'Hare International Airport. The holding pattern took it through clouds that contained freezing drizzle. As water droplets hit the airplane's wings they turned to ice. Like many commuters, the ATR-72 had deicing boots—rubber bladders on the leading edges of the wings that could be expanded to break off the ice. But a ridge of ice built up on the wings behind the boots. The ice ridge affected the airstream flowing over the wing and caused "a sudden and unexpected" movement of one of the ailerons, the safety board found. Before the pilots could react, the airplane rolled into a steep, high-speed dive. The plane slammed into a soybean field in Roselawn, Indiana, killing all sixty-eight aboard.

Certification Process Was Flawed

All civilian airplanes must be approved for flight by the Federal Aviation Administration. Among other things, an airplane must pass tests on its ability to fly in the conditions it was designed for. This approval is called certification. In this crash of the ATR-72, the NTSB made many findings and recommendations. One faulted the French airplane maker Avions de Transport Regional and French aviation authorities for not passing on information they had about the airplane's behavior in icing conditions. The NTSB also said the FAA contributed to the accident by not checking the ATR-72 more closely when it certified its use by United States airlines. Looking beyond this crash, the NTSB said the FAA's process for certifying aircraft, its rules for flight in icing conditions, and the icing information it publishes were not adequate.

In response to the crash, the FAA launched a three-phase plan to improve safety in in-flight icing conditions. The first phase set new rules for the ATR-72. The FAA banned ATR-72s from flying in known or forecast icing conditions in the United States until they could be equipped with better deicing boots. The plan's second phase was to screen other airplane types similar to the ATR-72 for a tendency to roll out of control in severe icing. The third phase would look at all aspects of certifying aircraft for flight in icing conditions. This would include new research on technologies to detect and forecast icing conditions, and learning more about icing caused by freezing rain and drizzle.[21]

But the FAA was still working on its plan more than two years later when another commuter plane fell victim to in-flight icing. This time, the NTSB named the FAA itself as the cause.

Disaster Does Not Wait

Icing claimed another commuter plane on January 9, 1997. Comair Flight 3272, an Embraer EMB-120, was descending toward the Detroit Metropolitan Wayne County Airport when it suddenly plunged to the ground. It crashed near Monroe, Michigan. None

An engineer measures ice on the leading edge of a wing section in the Icing Research Tunnel at NASA's Lewis Research Center, Cleveland, Ohio.

of the flight's three crew members or twenty-six passengers survived.

The NTSB concluded that a thin, rough layer of ice had built up on the wings. The ice apparently went unnoticed by the pilots because they had the autopilot engaged. With their hands off the controls, they could not feel the gradual changes in the airplane's handling. Before they knew anything was wrong, the plane suddenly rolled out of control and went into a dive.[22]

The FAA released its in-flight icing plan in April 1997. But in 1998, the NTSB said Comair 3272 crashed mainly because the FAA had not acted earlier. It said the cause of the crash was "the FAA's failure to establish adequate aircraft certification standards for flight in icing conditions." The statement said its investigation had found that "despite the accumulated lessons of several major accidents, the FAA failed to adopt a systematic, proactive approach" to certifying commuter planes like the EMB-120 and the ATR-72.[23]

The NTSB wanted the FAA to act much sooner to set safer standards. The FAA has developed a far-reaching plan to keep air travelers safe when icing threats loom.

But the plan came too late to help those on Comair 3272.

5

Mechanical Failure

Airplanes are very reliable machines. Most accidents result from human error, not mechanical failure. But airplanes are no better than the people who design, build, and maintain them. Seemingly small errors can cause big problems or even lead to disaster. The proper practices must be used to inspect and repair airplanes and their parts. New techniques must be devised to keep airplanes in good shape as they age. Proper airplane design, manufacturing, and maintenance are important issues in air safety.

These issues are not new. They are as

old as the first airplanes. And a tragic experience in the 1950s showed they still remained in the jet age.

Comet Started Jet Travel

In 1952, the British-built De Havilland Comet seemed to be streaking into the future. It was the world's first jet airliner, and it marked a dramatic breakthrough in commercial aviation. While the rest of the world trundled along in slow, shaking, propeller-powered airplanes, the Comet whooshed passengers across the sky with smooth, powerful turbojets.

"At a stroke it doubled the speed of air travel to 500 mph, and introduced a simultaneous quantum leap in the comfort of travel," wrote Nicholas Faith in *Black Box*.[1]

To Britain, battered from World War II, it was a source of national pride and an important chance to take a worldwide lead in the airliner business.

The Comet made its first commercial flight on May 2, 1952. Passengers and the press marveled at its speed, its comfort, and sweeping views out its large, square windows with gracefully rounded corners.

The airplane was designed to cruise above 30,000 feet—higher than Mount Everest. This carried passengers above most bad weather, and its jet engines ran more efficiently in the thin air. Passengers and crew traveled in pressurized comfort. But the relative pressure on the hull—the difference between the inside and outside air pressure—was greater with the high-flying Comet than with any other previous airliner. Pressurizing and depressurizing the hull with every takeoff and landing put stresses on it that no other airliner had experienced.

There were several mishaps with the Comet during its first year of regular flights. But its most serious problem appeared exactly one year after the airliner entered service. On May 2, 1953, a British Overseas Airways Corporation (BOAC) Comet went down in India. It plunged to earth six minutes after taking off from Calcutta. The airplane had encountered a thunderstorm with high winds. The graceful jet broke apart in midair.

The disasters continued. On January 10, 1954, a BOAC Comet exploded just as it reached cruising altitude. BOAC grounded its Comets while the airline and the manufacturer probed the accident. De Havilland suspected a problem with the engines—they were built into the wings near the fuselage—and made numerous changes to prevent fires or explosions. BOAC resumed Comet flights in late March.

But two weeks afterward, on April 8, another Comet fell out of the sky off the coast of Italy. Speculation on the causes ranged from sabotage to flying saucers.[2]

The British government grounded the airplanes and assigned the task of solving the mystery to the Royal Aircraft Establishment—Britain's national aeronautical research center.

Hidden Hazard: Metal Fatigue

Investigators studied airplane wreckage and the bodies of the victims dredged up from the seafloor.

All signs pointed to an abrupt, explosive loss of pressure, followed by the breakup of the airplane. But there was no evidence of a bomb. Instead, investigators found the telltale signs of metal fatigue—places where metal had weakened and cracked from wear. What had caused it?

The investigators already had a suspicion. While the Comet's remains were being examined, a huge water tank was built—one big enough to hold a

The dripless bubbler is used here by co-developer Thadd Patton to inspect an aircraft skin. The bubbler was developed at Iowa State University's Center for Nondestructive Evaluation. It permits ultrasonic scans over large surface protrusions, such as buttonhead rivets installed by the airline industry in response to the Aloha Airlines roof incident.

Comet's entire fuselage. A plane was put in the tank. Its wings stuck out through watertight seals. The tank was flooded, and the cabin was pumped full of water to the same pressure it would experience cruising at 36,000 feet. The cabin was kept pressurized for a few minutes, depressurized, then pressurized again—time after time, to simulate repeated flights. At the same time, its wings were flexed up and down with jacks to mimic the flexing of wings in flight.

After the equivalent of 9,000 flying hours, it happened: A three-by-eight-foot section of the cabin split open. "Only the watery embrace in which it was held prevented the cabin from blowing itself to bits," Derek D. Dempster wrote in *Tale of the Comet*.[3]

In the wreckage, the cabin roof had the same kind of split. Investigators found that the stresses on the hull had been concentrated in the small, rounded corners of the airplane's big windows.

The Comet was on the cutting edge of technology. Investigators concluded its weakness lay not in bad design work but in the limits of knowledge about metal fatigue. The Comet was redesigned, and De Havilland produced the Comet Four with tougher skin and smaller, rounded windows. But tragedy had tarnished its gleaming reputation, and other jets took over the airliner market.

Jumbo Jets Raise the Stakes

The Comet introduced the benefits and hazards of commercial jet flight in the 1950s. Likewise, jumbo jets in the late 1960s and early 1970s introduced the efficiency of airplanes that could carry hundreds of passengers—and raised the stakes for air safety. The crash of a single Boeing 747, Lockheed L-1011, or McDonnell Douglas DC-10 could take hundreds of lives.

In the 1970s, mechanical failures in two jumbo jets caused two of the worst air disasters ever. In each case, a single mechanical failure led to a chain of failures.

Although their causes were unrelated, both involved one of the world's biggest airliners—the McDonnell Douglas DC-10. The DC-10 had just been introduced in 1970. Because of these two crashes, its reputation suffered almost as badly as the Comet's. Wrote Bill Yenne in *The World's Worst Aircraft*, "These disasters gave the DC-10 the image of being the *Titanic* of the airways."[4]

Turkish Airlines Flight 981 was climbing from Orly Airport in France on March 3, 1974, when its rear cargo door blew off. It caused a sudden loss of pressure in the cargo space under the floor of the passenger cabin. The floor collapsed and the cabin lost pressure. The sudden loss of pressure also damaged control links to the elevator, rudder, and engines. Out of control, the giant jet nosed into a dive and hit the ground at almost 500 miles per hour. It exploded in a huge fireball. All 346 people aboard were killed, including six who were blown out when the plane lost pressure. At the time, it was the deadliest accident in aviation history.

Deadly Design Flaws

Investigators found a baggage handler had not latched the cargo door properly. But instead of simply blaming the baggage handler, investigators focused on the door's poor design. Most doors on jetliners opened inward; when it was closed, cabin pressure would hold it in place even if it were not latched properly. The DC-10's rear cargo door opened outward; if it were not latched properly, cabin pressure could force it open. The latches were set electrically, but they could become jammed. The door had a lever that was to be used to lock the latches in place, but if the latches jammed and force was used on the lever, it would merely bend parts inside the door without securing the latches.

Tragically, it was not the first time the door's design had been questioned. A similar door failure and floor collapse had happened to an American Airlines DC-10 leaving Detroit in June 1972. In that case, the crew was able to wrestle the plane back to the ground with no loss of life. The safety board had recommended the FAA order several changes in the design, but the FAA had decided to issue service bulletins instead. These described needed changes in the door design, but they did not carry the force of law. They put less pressure on airlines to act quickly.

Not all of the changes had been made to the door on Flight 981. After that crash, the FAA ordered a redesign of the cargo door. It also ordered improvements to cargo doors on two other jumbo jets, the Boeing 747 and the Lockheed L-1011. And it ordered passenger floors to be reinforced and venting improved to prevent them from collapsing if the cargo hold lost pressure.[5]

Safety Idea Downs Jet

The second DC-10 disaster came on May 25, 1979. Just as American Airlines Flight 191 was taking off from O'Hare Airport in Chicago, its number 1 engine and the pylon that held the engine to the bottom of the left wing broke off. The wounded jet continued to climb to about 325 feet above the ground, then rolled onto its left side and pitched down. It smashed into the ground, scattering pieces across an open field and a trailer park. Tons of jet fuel erupted in a ball of fire. The crash killed all 271 people on the plane and another two on the ground.[6] As this book was written, it stood as the deadliest air crash ever on United States soil.

The loss of an engine was not what caused the crash, investigators concluded. The crew could have flown the plane safely on the remaining engines—one under the right wing and one in the tail. But when the mounting pylon broke off, the engine went over the top of the wing and tore off a three-foot section of its leading edge. It also damaged part of the flight-control and stall-warning system in that part of the wing. As a result, the left wing stalled at a higher speed than normal, but the damaged stall warning system did not signal the crew. When it stalled, the wing lost lift and dipped, which made the plane suddenly roll to the left. It caught the crew by surprise, and there was not enough time to right the plane before it hit the ground.

Investigators traced the cause of the accident to a maintenance practice that had put a long crack in the engine pylon. It had weakened the structure just enough for the takeoff forces to break it.[7]

During maintenance work on the pylon, the standard practice was to remove the engine first, then the pylon. The airline had found it was quicker to remove the pylon from the wing with the engine attached, using a cradle mounted on a forklift. The airline thought it actually increased safety, because it eliminated the need to disconnect and reconnect many fuel lines and electrical cables between the engine and the pylon. Even the FAA had approved it.

But crash investigators found the procedure made it all too easy to put stresses on the mounting areas. The stresses could start cracks that would slowly spread. Checks of other DC-10s found similar cracks in the same locations. The FAA grounded all DC-10s for more than a month while the entire fleet was checked. Later, the FAA ordered new maintenance procedures.[8]

Aging Aircraft

Airplanes get old, but their age is not counted in calendar years. An airplane's age is measured by how many thousands of hours it has been flown and how many flights it has made—or what aviation specialists call flight cycles. An airliner with many flight cycles has been pressurized and depressurized a lot of times. Hours and flight cycles are mainly what "age" an airplane.

What is wrong with an old airplane? If it is well maintained, not a thing. But an incident in 1988 dramatically showed what can go wrong when aging signs are ignored.

An Airplane Blows Its Top

On April 28, 1988, Aloha Airlines Flight 243 was hopping across the Hawaiian Islands on its usual route. The Boeing 737 had made three trips around the islands already that morning. At 1:25 P.M., it took off on the leg from Hilo to Honolulu with ninety-five people aboard.

As the airplane leveled off to cruise at 24,000 feet, the pilots heard a sudden, loud "clap" or "whooshing" sound followed by wind noise behind them.[9] The copilot's head was jerked backward, and she saw pieces of debris floating in the cockpit. The captain looked back and saw that the cockpit door was missing. Through the gaping doorway where the first-class cabin ceiling should have been he saw blue sky instead.

Flight 243 had just blown its top. Weakened by frequent pressurization cycles, the cabin could no longer contain the air pressure. It let go with an explosive blast. Eighteen feet of cabin skin, from the back of the cockpit to the front edge of the wing, blew away. The passengers suddenly found themselves staring at the open sky, four and a half miles

The heavily damaged Aloha Airlines Flight 243 shortly after landing at Kahului, Hawaii.

above the Pacific Ocean, gasping for breath and blasted by jet-speed wind.

One of the plane's three flight attendants was immediately swept away to her death. Another was seriously injured by flying debris. The third attendant was able to crawl up and down the aisle to help passengers and try to calm them down.

The pilots put on their oxygen masks and started an emergency descent. The wind was so noisy they had to communicate with hand signals. They also had trouble talking to air traffic controllers over the radio. Below 10,000 feet, they could take off their oxygen masks. The captain slowed the plane and made a gentle turn for an emergency landing at Maui. One of the jet's two engines quit on final approach, but the captain succeeded in landing the plane.

On the ground, Aloha Flight 243 was a shocking sight. Passengers could be seen through the gaping hole, still strapped to their seats—terrified, some of them injured, but alive. Incredibly, the flight attendant swept out of the plane was the only person killed.

The NTSB blamed metal fatigue. But it also said the airline should have been aware of telltale cracks in the structure and should have had a better maintenance program, especially in view of the high number of pressurization cycles its planes experienced as they hopped from island to island.[10]

Airline Fleet Is Aging

Aloha Flight 243 drew special attention to the 737. It is one of the world's most commonly used jet airliners, and it is used on short routes that rapidly build up flight cycles. The FAA has continued to study the aging of 737s, occasionally issuing orders aimed at improving inspections or maintenance practices. In October 1997, for example, the FAA ordered repairs to fix cracks and strengthen the fuselage skin in sixteen 737s that had more than seventy thousand flight cycles. It also ordered more frequent inspections of another seventeen 737s with more than sixty thousand flight cycles. In 1998, it proposed another order that would require inspections of more than twenty-eight hundred Boeing 737s for cracks that could cause sudden pressure loss.

But Aloha Flight 243 also got safety experts thinking more broadly about the issue of aging aircraft. While it is inaccurate to judge an airplane by its years, the average age of a fleet is meaningful. As a fleet gets older, it is likely that more of its planes have seen a lot of use. And America's airline fleet is getting older. In 1988, the United States airline industry had thirty-seven hundred large airplanes, with an average age of 12.7 years. Ten years later, the number of planes had grown to fifty-four hundred and the average age to 15.8 years. By 2008, the United States fleet is expected to have an average age of eighteen to twenty years.[11]

The same is true for military fleets. After Aloha Flight 243, the FAA, Department of Defense, and NASA joined forces to research aging aircraft issues. They enlisted the help of universities and the aircraft industry. Most of the work focused on the airframe—fuselage, wings, and so on. In 1998, FAA administrator Jane Garvey announced a new plan to study aging in other parts. "We've learned that aging affects more than the airframe. In recent months, we've learned much more about nonstructural systems—electrical wiring, in particular," she said at a conference on aging aircraft. She added, "We may not be able to reverse the aging process, but we can make it safe."[12]

6

Security

Airport and airline officials are serious about security. Hundreds of people have died in aircraft disasters caused by terrorists, hijackers, or disturbed individuals. Joking about weapons or bombs is a good way to be detained at an airport if not arrested and charged with a federal crime.

Some people have learned this the hard way. One was Richard Allan Josephson of Wilmington, Delaware. He said fear of flying and depressing news about a friend's illness prompted him to down several alcoholic drinks before boarding a USAir flight in Philadelphia on October 13, 1996.

When a flight attendant picked up his carry-on bag to put it in an overhead storage bin, he said, "Gee, be careful, that's where I keep my pipe bombs."[1]

The attendant did not hear him, but a passenger did. She alerted the flight attendant who notified the captain that there might be a bomb on board the plane. By that time, Josephson had taken some pills and fallen asleep, and the crew could not awaken him. The flight was bound for Los Angeles, but the captain could not take a chance that a bomb was on his plane; there were 117 people on board. The jet made an emergency landing at Dayton International Airport in Ohio. The crew inflated emergency slides to get people off the plane quickly. Eight people suffered injuries sliding down the chutes, including one who suffered a broken leg.

But Josephson was still sleeping. When a Dayton firefighter finally roused him, Josephson said he had thirteen sticks of dynamite in his bag and a remote-control detonator in his pocket.

No bomb was found, and Josephson later said he was joking. But it was not funny to U.S. District Judge Walter Rice, in whose court Josephson later pleaded guilty to a charge of "endangering the safety of an aircraft."[2]

A bomb in an airplane is "one area that is simply not joked about," Rice said. Noting that Josephson's joke caused people to be hurt, the judge sentenced him to six months in prison and one hundred hours of community service, and ordered him to repay the airline $40,653 that the incident cost it.[3]

Security Is Increasing

Aviation officials have good reason to take bomb threats seriously. Bombing and hijacking of civilian airplanes are almost as old as commercial aviation itself. Over the decades, attacks on airliners have prompted ever tighter security methods. Passengers must go through metal detectors and have their bags X-rayed before they are permitted to board airplanes. New technologies are being used to peer into baggage with greater detail and sniff for traces of explosive chemicals. Specially trained dogs are also used to sniff baggage for explosives. Federal air marshals, dressed in plain clothes but armed, travel secretly on some flights. Computer programs sift through airline reservation databases to single out suspicious travelers for closer scrutiny. Critics say some security measures are too expensive and take away too much privacy while providing little more security.

Bombings, Gunfire Down Planes

The first confirmed bombing of a commercial airplane involved a United Airlines Boeing 247 on October 10, 1933. The airplane was carrying seven people from Cleveland to Chicago when a nitroglycerin bomb blew off its tail. All aboard died. Although they learned what caused the blast, authorities never learned enough about it to charge anyone.[4]

Airplanes are attacked, hijacked, or sabotaged for different reasons. For example, the FBI believes a jet was blown up on May 22, 1962, by a man who wanted to commit suicide and let his wife collect his life insurance payment. The Continental Airlines Boeing 707 broke apart in the air and crashed near Unionville, Missouri, killing all forty-five people aboard. The FBI determined that a dynamite bomb had been hidden in a used-towel bin in the lavatory. Bombings had entered the jet age.[5]

A disgruntled former USAir employee was blamed for the crash of a Pacific Southwest Airlines jet on December 7, 1987. Flight 1771, a British Aerospace BAE-146-200, took off from Los Angeles for San Francisco with forty-three people on board.

Dogs are put to work checking luggage and cargo for explosives and contraband.

Among them were the recently fired USAir employee and his former supervisor. While the airplane was at 22,000 feet, the captain radioed air traffic controllers that there was gunfire in the cabin. Then the jet nosed over and plunged into a hillside near San Luis Obispo, smashing into small pieces.[6]

Investigators found the passenger had left a "goodbye message" with friends and borrowed a pistol. Nobody checked him when he boarded; with his airline employee identification, he was allowed to bypass airport security checkpoints. The debris yielded the gun with six empty shells in it, a threatening note the employee had written to his supervisor, and the cockpit voice recorder with sounds of a scuffle and gunfire on its tape. The safety board concluded that inadequate security contributed to the crash. A few months later, the Department of Transportation told Congress it would tighten security rules for airport and airline employees at the nation's busiest airports.

Hijacker Becomes a Legend

One hijacker became a folk legend when he seized a Northwest Orient Airlines plane on December 24, 1971. A man whose ticket identified him only as D. B. Cooper boarded the Boeing 727 in Portland wearing a business suit and dark glasses. Once the plane was airborne, Cooper told a flight attendant he had a bomb in his briefcase. He demanded $200,000 in $20 bills, and four parachutes. The plane landed in Seattle, where the money and parachutes were put on board. Cooper released the flight's thirty-six passengers and all but three crew members, then ordered the jet to take off for Reno, Nevada.

When the plane landed, Cooper was gone and the rear exit door under the tail was open. Obviously, Cooper had donned one of the parachutes and leaped out. The bills had been marked, but no trace of Cooper or the money surfaced for years. In 1980, children playing along the Columbia River near Vancouver found a few thousand dollars of the loot partially buried in a riverbank. Since then, some people have speculated the money washed up there after Cooper died from the jump. Others think Cooper might have survived and stashed some of the money along the river.[7] The hijacking drew so much attention it resulted in books and a Hollywood film—as well as more than a dozen similar hijacking attempts over the next several years. None succeeded.[8]

Political Hijackers

While some hijackings are for money, most have been for political reasons. In the 1940s and 1950s, many individuals or small groups seized planes in communist countries to escape to freedom. Cuba became the focus of hijackings in the late 1960s, although many were by people trying to flee to Cuba from North or South America. More than a score took place or were attempted in 1968, and they continued at a frequent rate through the early 1970s. Even later, some years saw more than one attempt each year. Many who got to Cuba wound up in jail, anyway.

The threat of hijackings prompted a new security program: federal air marshals. They first began flying on U.S. airplanes in 1962 to counter the Cuban hijacking threat. The program has been expanded over the years, although how many marshals there are and what flights they are on is classified. The thought of a shootout in an airliner cabin during a flight might make some people nervous—passengers as well as airline officials. However, no air marshal has encountered a hijacking. The possibility of confronting a trained, armed marshal is believed to have discouraged many hijacking attempts. Metal detectors and baggage X-raying also have made it much more difficult to sneak a weapon onto a plane.[9] No hijacking attempt has taken place on a flight in the United States since 1991, according to the FAA.[10]

Terrorists

Many airliner assaults have been terrorist acts. One of the most bizarre, although not the deadliest, was the stunning hijacking of four jet airliners in September 1970.

Between September 6 and September 12, Palestinian guerrillas seized a Pan Am 747 with 170 people aboard in Amsterdam, the Netherlands; a TWA 707 as it left Frankfurt, West Germany, with 151 aboard; a Swissair DC-8 as it left Zurich, Switzerland, with 155 aboard; and a British Overseas Airways Super VC-10 out of Bahrain with 114 aboard. The

747 was flown to Cairo, Egypt, where the guerrillas evacuated the plane and blew it up. The 707, DC-8, and Super VC-10 were landed on the Jordanian desert, where they, too, were evacuated and then blown up. The hostages were later released. A fifth hijacking attempt failed, and one of the two hijackers was fatally shot.[11]

Lost Airliner Shot Down

Some airliners have been attacked by foreign governments—not just in wartime, but even when the governments were supposedly at peace.

During the Cold War, the borders of the Soviet Union and Soviet-controlled nations of Eastern Europe were largely closed to outsiders. Western nations knew the Soviet Union was building bombers, missiles, and nuclear weapons; they feared the possibility of a massive surprise attack. The United States flew daring spy plane missions along communist countries' borders and, sometimes, deep into their airspace. Besides trying to see what the Soviets were up to, the spy planes also probed for weak points in Soviet air defenses. Some of those spy planes were shot down. So, too, were some civilian ones.

The most infamous act of this kind happened on September 1, 1983, when a Soviet jet fighter shot down a Korean Air Lines jet carrying 269 people. KAL 007, a Boeing 747, was on its way from New York to Seoul, South Korea. It stopped to refuel and change crews in Anchorage, Alaska, then took off for Seoul. In the darkness of night, it drifted off course and entered Soviet airspace over the Sea of Japan. A Soviet fighter jet intercepted the 747 and followed it for twenty minutes. Then it fired two missiles that sent the giant airplane into the sea. All aboard died.[12]

The downing of KAL 007 sparked an international storm of protest. The Soviet Union at first claimed the jumbo jet was a spy plane. In fact, a United States RC-135 reconnaissance jet, a Boeing plane that looks a lot like an airliner, had been in the area earlier. The Soviet Union refused to turn over the flight data and cockpit voice recorders. After the Soviet Union's collapse, the Commonwealth of Independent States, made up of countries that had been a part of the Soviet Union, released a report in 1993 that largely supported the Soviet action.[13]

United States Shoots Down Iranian Airliner

In 1988, the United States had to defend its own military attack on a civilian aircraft.

The stage had been set more than a year earlier. Iraq and Iran were at war, and oil tankers from Kuwait hauling oil through the narrow Strait of Hormuz were at risk of attack by both nations. The United States Navy began convoying the tankers under its protection. In May 1987, an Iraqi fighter jet struck the *Stark*, a frigate, with a missile Iraq claimed was fired accidentally. The missile killed thirty-seven United States sailors and nearly sank the *Stark*.

The incident made commanders edgy. They had

been warned to watch for Iranian military action around Independence Day, July 4, 1988. On the morning of July 3, the navy cruiser *Vincennes* was in a shootout with Iranian gunboats when an Iranian patrol aircraft came on the scene. At the same time, the *Vincennes*'s radar picked up another aircraft headed straight at the cruiser from an Iranian airport. Was the patrol plane guiding another jet on an attack run? The *Vincennes* broadcast several warnings to the plane; when it failed to turn away, the ship fired two surface-to-air missiles at it. The aircraft was hit, and it fell into the sea.

But the aircraft was not an attacker. It was Iran Air Flight 655, an Airbus A300 with 290 people on board. They all died.

The Navy blamed its error on atmospheric conditions that caused it to misidentify the aircraft. But data from the *Vincennes*'s defensive system indicated a civilian aircraft. It was not known why the Iranian crew did not heed the warnings. In 1996, the United States agreed to pay $60 million to families of the victims.

But the tragedy further damaged already bad relations between the United States and Iran. And memories of it resurfaced in 1996 after the crash of TWA 800 off New York. Witnesses to this fiery crash thought they had seen a streak of light before the jet exploded. Claims that a navy ship had accidentally shot down the airliner flashed across the Internet and surfaced in the news media. Investigators interviewed dozens of eyewitnesses and divers collected more than 95 percent of the wreckage. Investigators said the evidence did not show the kinds of damage a missile would have caused.

Bomb Downs Jumbo Jet

Before 1988 was over, another major airliner fell victim to violence. On December 21, Pan Am Flight 103, a 747, was ripped apart by an explosion 31,000 feet above the town of Lockerbie, Scotland. Radar showed pieces fanning out over a wide area. Below, townspeople heard a rumble like thunder that grew quickly into a deafening roar. "The noise appeared to come from a meteor-like object which was trailing flame," Britain's Air Accidents Investigation Branch reported.[14]

The burning fuselage and wings smashed down on the town, digging huge craters. The wings exploded in a massive fireball that spread flames and burning debris to neighboring houses. All 259 people aboard the plane died, and eleven more on the ground perished. More than twenty homes were destroyed or damaged beyond repair.

Investigators found the remains of a radio-cassette player that had been fitted with an explosive. It had gone off in the forward cargo bay, blowing a large hole in the side of the jet and weakening the fuselage structure.

United States and British intelligence agents at first suspected Iran of an attack in revenge for the shootdown of Iran Air 655, but later they pinned the blame on two Libyan intelligence agents. Both the United States and the United Kingdom filed charges against them in 1991 and demanded that Libya turn them over for trial. Libya refused for years but eventually said it would allow a Scottish court to try the suspects in a third country. In 1998, the United States and Britain offered to allow the trial to be held in the Netherlands. Libya had not turned over its agents as this book went to press.

Security Concerns in the 1990s

The bombing of Pan Am 103 caused widespread public concern about security. Congress responded with the Aviation Security Improvement Act of 1990, which required the FAA to develop standards for equipment that could be used to detect explosives in baggage. In 1996, suspicions of terrorism—later ruled out—in the explosion of TWA 800 set off a fresh wave of concern. Keith O. Fultz, an official with the General Accounting Office, summed it up in a congressional hearing on September 11, 1996:

> The 1988 terrorist bombing of Pan Am flight 103, which killed 270 people, and the more recent, but as yet unexplained, explosion of TWA flight 800, have shaken the public's confidence in the safety and security of air travel.[15]

Fultz said the threat of international and domestic terrorism was increasing, and aviation was an attractive target. He also warned in a later hearing that, while aviation security was tighter than ever, "Nearly every major aspect of the system . . . has weaknesses that could be exploited [by terrorists]."[16]

In conjunction with the GAO report, the Gore

Commission urged security action on several fronts. Most were things the FAA was already working on, but Congress boosted funding to speed them up. Many involved better internal operations, but some directly affected passengers:

- *Explosives detection for baggage.* Several years of development efforts led to new machines that could peer into baggage and see small amounts of explosives. The FAA demanded machines that could scan bags quickly, spot tiny devices, yet trigger few "false alarms," which would bog down the process. The latest machines, such as the CTX-5000 series by InVision Technologies, Inc., use technology developed for medical use to examine the insides of bags and packages.

- *Trace detection devices.* These are machines that can detect extremely small traces of explosive chemicals. Some devices can be used to check suspicious items around the airport; others would be walk-through devices that scan passengers' clothing; and still others would check for residues on tickets or boarding cards passengers have handled.

- *Hardened cargo containers.* The FAA bought one hundred cargo containers designed to contain the kind of explosion that caused the destruction of Pan Am 103 over Lockerbie, Scotland. It planned to let airlines use them to see how well they stood up to everyday wear and tear.

- *Automated passenger profiling.* Northwest Airlines developed a system funded by the FAA called Computer Assisted Passenger Screening (CAPS). It uses information in its reservation system to identify passengers who should get closer screening, such as making sure their bags are on the same flight or screening their bags for explosives. Other airlines were beginning to phase in the system in 1998.

- *Passenger-bag matching.* Airlines are already required to make sure no passenger's bags are

InVision Technologies' bomb detection system uses both X-ray and CT (computed tomography) technology to screen baggage for explosives.

flown on an international flight unless the passenger is also on the flight. The FAA is expanding this practice to include domestic flights.[17]

But all this technology is expensive. For example, the new explosives-detection machines cost hundreds of thousands of dollars apiece, and each of the busiest airports may need several. Congress approved $144 million for aviation security in 1997 and $100 million in 1998.[18] But that amount "represents a fraction of the estimated billions of dollars required to enhance the security of air travel," Gerald L. Dillingham, the GAO's chief of transportation issues, told a Senate hearing in March 1997.[19]

Some air safety experts say the money could be better spent elsewhere. In 1997, the Flight Safety Foundation blasted the security-spending boost as a "knee-jerk" reaction to the TWA 800 accident. "There is little evidence of security breaches in the North American continent, and the idea that the downing of TWA Flight 800 was caused by terrorism has largely been discounted," said Stuart Matthews, the foundation's president, chairman, and chief executive. He argued the money should be spent on intelligence, to spot terrorists before they try to board planes, and on other safety issues: "It would be better for these funds to be applied toward overcoming the recognized causes of accidents, rather than conjectured problems."[20]

There is also a question of privacy. How much are passengers willing to give up in order to fly? Will passenger profiling violate the civil rights of some citizens by singling them out for tighter security? Will the public tolerate extra screenings that sample passengers' clothing or skin for traces of explosives? Cathal L. Flynn, the FAA's associate administrator for civil aviation security, told a congressional hearing in 1998 that "the FAA has taken great care to protect civil liberties."

A review by the United States Department of Justice found CAPS "complies with the constitutional standards that guarantee equal protection and prohibit unreasonable searches and seizures" and that "CAPS does not involve any invasion of passengers' personal privacy," Flynn said.[21]

No security measures will be perfect. The ability of machines to catch the tiniest of explosives must be balanced with the need to board passengers, baggage, and cargo quickly. The quality of training for human operators and their ability to work quickly without missing anything are also factors. The industry journal *Aviation Week & Space Technology* summed up the security dilemma with a quote from an unnamed airport operator: "You will be perfectly safe only when there are no flights."[22]

7

Air Safety in Perspective

Like a blunt spear point, an airliner slices through the sky at more than five hundred miles per hour. It is a massive metal sculpture: wings and body blend into a smooth, slippery shape. It is a radical design, but its most radical feature is inside: seats for up to 800 passengers on two decks, twice the capacity of traditional jumbo jets.

This is a vision of the future that engineers call a "blended-wing-body transport." Researchers at the former McDonnell Douglas Corporation (now Boeing Company), NASA research centers, and several universities have studied this concept. They think it might be a way to relieve some of the pressures facing commercial aviation. It could haul the same number of passengers as two jumbo jets, but it would be more fuel-efficient and cause less air pollution. It would also mean one aircraft instead of two for air traffic controllers to contend with.[1]

But a crash of one of these superjumbos would increase the scale of an accident to epic proportions. Titanic might be a better word; the human toll of such a crash could be half that of the ocean liner *Titanic*, which claimed 1,513 lives when it sank after hitting an iceberg in 1912.[2]

Superjumbos lie years in the future, but air traffic growth is already straining the capacities of airports, airways, and air traffic control systems. Aviation authorities and the commercial aviation industry face serious challenges to maintaining air safety. The Gore Commission stressed the importance of not just keeping the accident rate steady, but also driving it even lower. "Unless that rate is reduced, the actual number of accidents will grow as traffic increases," the commission reported. It cited a 1994 study by Boeing that if current trends continued, by the year 2015 an airliner would crash somewhere in the world nearly every week.[3] Obviously, air safety is not a passing concern.

The Importance of Air Safety

Air safety is important because it affects people's lives and America's economy. In the United States,

This blended-wing-body aircraft is a concept for an airliner that could carry 800 passengers more than 7,000 miles. Researchers from NASA, the aircraft industry, and universities developed the concept as a way of accommodating the growth in air travel expected in the next century.

airlines logged 9.5 million scheduled flights in 1997 and carried 625 million passengers. Economically, air travel is important to the United States because it is a world leader in the airline market. Airlines around the world buy U.S.-built airplanes and air traffic control systems. The commercial aviation industry was worth $300 billion to the United States in 1996.

Air safety depends to a large degree on the efforts of two agencies. The Federal Aviation Administration certifies aircraft and pilots, provides air traffic control, and enforces air safety rules. It is also the FAA's job to assist and promote air transportation. As a result, its actions require a balancing act between air safety and the costs its rules impose on airline companies. The National Transportation Safety Board investigates air crashes and recommends ways to prevent future crashes. It has no power to enforce its recommendations, but its advice is usually followed.

The FAA does not always do what the NTSB recommends. Sometimes this is because the FAA wants to be sure that whatever action it takes will be the best way to increase safety. Sometimes it is because the FAA thinks a recommendation, if turned into a requirement, would cost the airlines too much for the amount of safety it would add.

Public pressure can spur safety changes, but it sometimes takes a major crash to focus public attention on a safety issue.

Safety Is a Global Issue

Air safety is not just a national issue but a global one. International flights are subject to the air traffic control rules of more than one nation. They use airports built and operated by different nations. Pilots and air traffic controllers from different nations must be able to communicate. The United States works closely with the International Civil Aviation Organization. Based in Montreal, Canada, its members include 185 countries. It works to standardize rules governing air transportation.

Improving safety requires improvements in training and technology and continuing research. It all costs money and takes time. Experts sometimes disagree on the most effective way to reduce accidents. Below are the key areas where efforts are being made to improve air safety.

Modernization

In the 1990s, air traffic growth was reaching the limits of what the air traffic control system could handle. The FAA has been working on a modernization plan since 1981. It involves replacing equipment and software around the United States with advanced systems that allow controllers to handle more traffic without reducing safety. But the systems have proved difficult to develop, and the FAA did a poor job of managing the expensive programs. Projects ran over budget and behind schedule. The FAA now expects the modernization plan to cost at least $35 billion by the end of 2003.

Human Error

Most accidents result from human error. In fact, studies have found that most accidents involve chains of errors by more than one person.

Airlines have adopted a training method commonly called crew resource management (CRM). It teaches crew members to act as a team, sharing information and checking one another for errors.

Most human-error accidents involve controlled-flight-into-terrain (CFIT) accidents, where a properly operating airplane is flown into the ground. Technology helps guard against CFIT accidents, but technology is not perfect. The newest system is called

The newest flight simulators incorporate computer-generated images to realistically duplicate flight conditions.

the Enhanced Ground Proximity Warning System. It uses navigation signals and an electronic map to tell when the airplane is approaching dangerous terrain. In 1998, the FAA proposed a rule that would require airlines to have the systems in their airplanes. Although the FAA estimated it would cost the industry more than $400 million, it predicted the industry would save far more—more than $5 billion. Most airlines decided to buy the new systems without waiting for an order.

Weather

A variety of aids already helps pilots get through, over, or around bad weather. But the earth's weather system is extremely complex.

It is important to develop technologies that can predict dangerous weather and get the information to pilots. This involves important decisions on which technologies to spend money on and how quickly to put new systems into operation. It is also important to make sure airplanes are properly equipped for the weather they fly in, and crews trained in the correct procedures for dangerous weather.

Mechanical Failure

Airplanes are very reliable, but they are no better than the people who design, build, and maintain them. The FAA sometimes depends on cooperation from the airlines to fix defects instead of ordering prompt action. Tragic accidents have spotlighted the need for careful maintenance practices.

Maintenance is a growing concern as America's airplane fleet grows older. In 1988, an airliner made "aging aircraft" a household term when an eighteen-foot section of its cabin roof peeled away in the middle of a flight. The explosion of TWA 800 raised concerns that old electrical wiring might have caused a spark that ignited fuel vapors. The FAA is working with other federal agencies, universities, and the airline industry to learn better ways to keep airplanes safe over years of regular use.

Security

Aviation officials have good reason to take bomb threats seriously. Over the decades, bombing and hijacking attacks on airliners have prompted ever tighter security methods until now even joking about it can bring time in jail.

Passengers must now go through metal detectors and have their bags X-rayed before they are permitted to board airplanes. New technologies are being put into use that can peer into baggage with greater detail and sniff for traces of explosive chemicals. In the future, computer programs may sift through airline-reservation databases to single out suspicious travelers for closer checks. Critics say these extra security measures are too expensive and take away too much privacy for little more security.

The Next Century

In 1901, Wilbur Wright predicted that men would not fly within his lifetime. Two years later, he and his brother, Orville Wright, made the world's first successful flights in a powered aircraft. Today, millions of people fly safely all over the world. The year 2003 will mark one hundred years of powered flight—a single century in which people turned the age-old dream of wings into a global transportation system. The challenge of the next century will not be to reach the sky but to keep air travel safe as it continues to grow.

Chapter Notes

Chapter 1. Disaster!

1. Federal Aviation Administration, "Reference Aircraft Accident TWA 800," transcript (Washington, D.C.: Federal Aviation Administration, July 29, 1996).

2. Ibid.

3. "Panel Summary: Investigation of Recorded Data," *Public Hearing: TWA Flight 800*, December 8–12, 1997, <http://www.ntsb.gov/events/twa800/recorded.htm> (March 22, 1999).

4. Jim Hall, "Chairman's Opening Statement," *Public Hearing: TWA Flight 800*, December 8–12, 1997, <http://www.ntsb.gov/Speeches/jh971208.htm> (March 22, 1999); Alfred W. Dickinson, "Statement of Investigator in Charge," *Public Hearing: TWA Flight 800*, December 8–12, 1997, <http://www.ntsb.gov/ Speeches/S971208.htm> (March 22, 1999).

5. Ibid.

6. Jim Hall, "Remarks Before the International Aviation Club," speech (Washington, D.C.: National Transportation Safety Board, January 21, 1998).

7. Jim Hall, "Chairman's Opening Statement."

8. National Transportation Safety Board, "Table 6: Accidents, Fatalities, and Accident Rates, 1982 through 1997, for U.S. Air Carriers Operating under 14 CFR 121, Scheduled Service," *Aviation Accident Statistics*, February 1998, <http://www.ntsb.gov/Aviation/Table6.htm> (March 22, 1999).

9. National Transportation Safety Board, "1997 U.S. Airline Fatalities Down Substantially from Previous Year; General Aviation Deaths Rise," news release (Washington, D.C.: National Transportation Safety Board, February 24, 1998).

10. National Transportation Safety Board, "Transportation Fatalities Hold Steady in 1997," news release (Washington, D.C.: National Transportation Safety Board, August 10, 1998).

11. Ibid.

12. National Transportation Safety Board, "Synopsis of Final Report, ValuJet 592 Accident Investigation," *Aviation Accident Synopses,* June 1997, <http://www.ntsb.gov/Aviation/DCA/ 96A054.htm> (March 22, 1999).

13. "Transcript released by the National Transportation Safety Board of ValuJet Flight 592 cockpit recordings," *Associated Press*, November 23, 1996.

14. William Langewiesche, "The Lessons of ValuJet 592," *The Atlantic Monthly*, March 1998, p. 84.

15. James T. McKenna, "Chain of Errors Downed ValuJet," *Aviation Week & Space Technology*, August 25, 1997, p. 34.

16. National Transportation Safety Board, "Synopsis of Final Report, ValuJet 592 Accident Investigation."

17. Jim Hall, "Testimony Before the Committee on Transportation and Infrastructure, Subcommittee on Aviation" (Washington, D.C., May 15, 1997).

18. Jim Loney, "ValuJet Crash Families Hit Air Regulators," *Reuters*, November 20, 1996.

19. Federal Aviation Administration, "This Is the FAA," *FAA Aviation Education Page*, 1998, <http://www.faa.gov/ education/documents/other/thisisfaa/this.pdf>, pp. 1, 13–15, (March 22, 1999).

20. Jim Hall, "Remarks Before the Second World Congress, Delft University of Technology, The Netherlands," speech (Washington, D.C.: National Transportation Safety Board, February 19, 1998).

21. Ibid.

22. Ibid.

23. Jim Hall, "Remarks Before the International Aviation Club."

24. Ibid.

25. Jim Hall, "Remarks Before the Second World Congress, Delft University of Technology, The Netherlands."

26. Lee Hamilton Sawyer, "Testimony Before the Committee on Transportation and Infrastructure, Subcommittee on Aviation" (Washington, D.C., May 15, 1997).

27. Al Gore et al., "Final Report to President Clinton," *White House Commission on Aviation Safety and Security*, February 12, 1997, Chapter 1, <http://www.aviationcommission.dot.gov/ 212fin~1.html> (March 22, 1999).

28. Ibid.

29. Al Gore, "Remarks by Vice-President Al Gore, International Conference on Aviation Safety and Security," *White House Commission on Aviation Safety and Security*, January 15, 1997, <http://www.aviationcommission.dot.gov/announce/ gwuconf2.html> (March 22, 1999).

30. Gore et al., "Final Report to President Clinton," Key Recommendations, Introduction.

31. "Gore Commission Proposals Are a Mixed Bag," *Aviation Week & Space Technology*, February 24, 1997, p. 82.

Chapter 2. From Gliders to Gridlock

1. Tom Crouch, *The Bishop's Boys: A Life of Wilbur and Orville Wright* (New York: W. W. Norton & Co., 1989), p. 213.

2. Ibid., p. 270.

3. William K. Kershner, *The Student Pilot's Flight Manual* (Ames: Iowa State University Press, 1979), pp. 3–9.

4. Kershner, pp. 93–94.

5. Crouch, p. 296.

6. Kershner, pp. 46–49.

7. Carl Solberg, *Conquest of the Skies: A History of Commercial Aviation in America* (Boston: Little, Brown & Co., 1979), p. 117.

8. National Transportation Safety Board, "Table 3: Passenger Injuries and Injury Rates, 1982 through 1987, for U.S. Air Carriers Operating under 14 CFR 121," *Aviation Accident Statistics*, February 1998, <http://www.ntsb.gov/ aviation/Stats.htm> (March 22, 1999).

9. International Civil Aeronautics Organization, "ICAO's Aims," *About ICAO*, n.d., <http://www.icao.org/cgi/goto. pl?icao/en/about.htm> (March 22, 1999).

10. National Civil Aviation Review Commission, *Avoiding Aviation Gridlock and Reducing the Accident Rate: A Consensus for Change* (Landover, Md.: TASC Department Warehouse, December 1997).

11. U.S. General Accounting Office, *Aviation Acquisition: A Comprehensive Strategy Is Needed for Cultural Change at FAA* (Washington, D.C.: U.S. Government Printing Office, August 22, 1996).

12. Ibid.

Chapter 3. Human Error

1. Robert L. Helmreich, "Managing Human Error in Aviation," *Scientific American*, May 1997, p. 62.

2. Shari Stamford Krause, *Aircraft Safety* (New York: McGraw-Hill, 1996), p. 1.

3. David Beaty, *The Naked Pilot* (Shrewsbury, England: Airlife, 1995), p. 27.

4. Al Gore et al., "Final Report to President Clinton," *White House Commission on Aviation Safety and Security*, February 12, 1997, Chapter 1, <http://www.aviationcommission.dot.gov/212fin~1. html> (March 22, 1999).

5. David Gero, *Aviation Disasters* (Sparkford, England: Patrick Stephens, 1996), pp. 142–143.

6. Ibid.

7. Ibid.

8. Beaty, *The Naked Pilot*, p. 84.

9. David Grayson, *Terror in the Skies* (Secaucus, N.J.: Citadel, 1988), pp. 26–40.

10. U.S. General Accounting Office, *FAA's Guidance and Oversight of Pilot Crew Resource Management Training Can Be Improved* (Washington, D.C.: U.S. Government Printing Office, November 1997), p. 3.

11. Helmreich, p. 67.

12. National Transportation Safety Board, *United Airlines Flight 232, McDonnell Douglas DC-10-10, Sioux Gateway Airport, Sioux City, Iowa*, Order No. PB90-910406 (Springfield, Va.: National Technical Information Service, November 1, 1990).

13. Helmreich, p. 65.

14. Ibid.

15. Stuart Matthews, "Commercial Airline Passengers Still Fly Safe Skies, FSF Emphasizes," news release (Alexandria, Va.: Flight Safety Foundation, July 17, 1997).

16. U.S. Office of Technology Assessment, *Safe Skies for Tomorrow* (Washington, D.C.: U.S. Government Printing Office, 1988), p. 166.

17. Grayson, pp. 89–98.

18. Federal Aviation Administration, "Notice of Proposed Rulemaking: Terrain Awareness and Warning System" (Washington, D.C.: Federal Aviation Administration, August 19, 1998).

19. *Controlled Flight into Terrain: American Airlines Flight 965, Boeing 757-223, N651AA, near Cali, Colombia, December 20, 1995*; Peter Ladkin, "AA965 Cali Accident Report," November 6, 1996, <http://members.aol.com/avcrash3/calirep.txt> (March 22, 1999).

20. Ibid.

21. Ibid.

22. Federal Aviation Administration, "Notice of Proposed Rulemaking."

23. Ibid.

24. AlliedSignal Commercial Avionics Systems, "American Airlines Buys $20 Million of Systems for Its Fleet," news release (Olathe, Kan.: AlliedSignal Commercial Avionics Systems, September 2, 1996).

25. Air Transport Association, "New Safety Equipment to Be Installed on 4,300 Aircraft," news release (Washington, D.C.: Air Transport Association, December 15, 1997).

26. Federal Aviation Administration, *1998 Federal Aviation Administration Strategic Plan* (Washington, D.C.: Federal Aviation Administration, May 20, 1998), p. 14.

Chapter 4. Weather

1. Federal Aviation Administration, *Physiological Training 1990* (Oklahoma City: Mike Monroney Aeronautical Center, 1990), p. 22.

2. Shari Stamford Krause, *Aircraft Safety* (New York: McGraw Hill, 1996), p. 209.

3. Ibid., pp. 209–210.

4. National Transportation Safety Board, *Eastern Airlines, Inc., Boeing 727-225, JFK International Airport, Jamaica, New York, June 24, 1975*, Order No. UB/B/104-76/008 (Springfield, Va.: National Technical Information Service, March 12, 1976).

5. Ibid.

6. Lane E. Wallace, *Airborne Trailblazer* (Washington, D.C.: National Aeronautics and Space Administration, 1994), pp. 56, 59.

7. Ibid.

8. John Monk and David Perlmutt, "Life-Saving Weather Radar Lags," *Charlotte Observer*, July 24, 1994, p. 1A.

9. Ibid.

10. James J. Haggerty, "Technology for Safer Skies," *Spinoff 1995* (Washington, D.C.: National Aeronautics and Space Administration, 1995).

11. National Research Council, "Weather Reports Should Become Higher Priority for Air Traffic Control," news release (Washington, D.C.: National Research Council, November 7, 1995).

12. Ibid.

13. Federal Aviation Administration, "FAA Selects Raytheon for New Weather Hazards Prediction System," news release (Washington, D.C.: Federal Aviation Administration, January 29, 1997).

14. U.S. General Accounting Office, *Aviation Acquisition: A Comprehensive Strategy Is Needed for Cultural Change at FAA* (Washington, D.C.: U.S. Government Printing Office, August 22, 1996).

15. Federal Aviation Administration, *Pilot Guide: Large Aircraft Ground Deicing*, Advisory Circular (AC) 120-58 (Washington, D.C.: U.S. Government Printing Office, May 19, 1994).

16. Krause, pp. 64–65.

17. Ibid., p. 66.

18. National Transportation Safety Board, *Air Florida, Inc., Boeing 737-222, N62AF, Collision with 14th Street Bridge*, Order No. PB82-910408 (Springfield, Va.: National Technical Information Service, August 10, 1982).

19. National Transportation Safety Board, *Takeoff Stall in Icing Conditions USAIR Flight 405, FOKKER F-28, N485US*, Order No. PB93-910402 (Springfield, Va.: National Technical Information Service, February 17, 1993).

20. Ibid.

21. Federal Aviation Administration, *FAA Inflight Aircraft Icing Plan* (Washington, D.C.: Department of Transportation, April 1997).

22. National Transportation Safety Board, *Abstract of Final Report, In-Flight Icing Encounter and Uncontrolled Collision with Terrain, Comair Flight 3272, Embraer EMB-120RT, N265CA, Monroe, Michigan, January 9, 1997* (Washington, D.C.: National Transportation Safety Board, August 27, 1998).

23. National Transportation Safety Board, "Safety Board Faults FAA Aircraft Certification Standards and Oversight in Michigan Commuter Plane Crash," news release (Washington, D.C.: National Transportation Safety Board, August 27, 1998).

Chapter 5. Mechanical Failure

1. Nicholas Faith, *Black Box: The Air-Crash Detectives—Why Air Safety Is No Accident* (London: Boxtree, 1996), p. 53.

2. Ibid., p. 56.

3. Derek D. Dempster, *Tale of the Comet* (New York: David McKay Company, Inc., 1958), p. 167.

4. Bill Yenne, *The World's Worst Aircraft* (New York: Marboro Books, 1990), p. 8.

5. David Gero, *Aviation Disasters* (Sparkford, England: Patrick Stephens, 1996), p. 126.

6. National Transportation Safety Board, *American Airlines, Inc., DC-10, N110AA, Chicago International Airport, Chicago IL, May 25, 1979*, Order No. UB/E/104-017 (Springfield, Va.: National Technical Information Service, December 21, 1979).

7. Ibid.

8. Gero, pp. 153–156.

9. National Transportation Safety Board, *Aloha Airlines, Flight 243, Boeing 737-200, N73711, Near Maui, Hawaii, April 28, 1989*, Order No. PB89-910405 (Springfield, Va.: National Technical Information Service, June 14, 1989).

10. Ibid.

11. Jane F. Garvey, "Remarks Prepared for Delivery, Second Joint NASA/FAA/DOD Conference on Aircraft Aging, Williamsburg, Virginia," speech (Washington, D.C.: Federal Aviation Administration, August 31, 1998).

12. Ibid.

Chapter 6. Security

1. Wes Hills, "Tab for Joke: $40,000, Prison Term," *Dayton Daily News*, February 26, 1998, p. 1A.

2. Ibid.

3. Ibid.

4. David Gero, *Flights of Terror* (Sparkford, England: Patrick Stephens, 1997), p. 10.

5. David Gero, *Aviation Disasters* (Sparkford, England: Patrick Stephens, 1996), pp. 48–49.

6. National Transportation Safety Board, "Scheduled 14 CFR 121 Operation of Pacific Southwest Airlines, Accident Occurred Dec-07-87 at San Luis Obispo, CA" (Synopsis), *Aviation Accident Synopses*, n.d., <http://www.ntsb.gov/aviation/DCA/88AA008.htm> (March 22, 1999).

7. Carl Sifakis, *Encyclopedia of American Crime* (New York: Facts on File, 1982), p. 172.

8. Gero, *Flights of Terror*, pp. 100–103.

9. James Ott, "Sky Marshals Reduce Hijacking Threat," *Aviation Week & Space Technology*, December 16, 1996, p. 26.

10. Cathal L. Flynn, associate administrator for civil aviation security, Federal Aviation Administration, "Statement," *House Committee on Transportation and Infrastructure, Subcommittee on Aviation Hearing*, May 14, 1998, <http://www.faa.gov/apa/testimony/51498tecf.htm> (March 22, 1999).

11. Gero, *Flights of Terror*, pp. 70–72.

12. Ibid., pp. 112–113.

13. Ibid.

14. U.K. Air Accidents Investigation Branch, *Report on the Accident to Boeing 747-121, N739PA at Lockerbie, Dumfriesshire, Scotland on 21 December 1988*, n.d., <http://www.open.gov.uk/aaib/n739pa.htm> (March 22, 1999).

15. Keith O. Fultz, "Testimony of Keith O. Fultz, Assistant Comptroller General, Resources, Community, and Economic Development Division," *House Committee on Transportation and Infrastructure, Subcommittee on Aviation Hearing*, September 11, 1996, <http://www.house.gov/transportation/aviation/avhearin/05-14-98/fultz.htm> (March 22, 1999).

16. Ibid.

17. U.S. Department of Transportation, *White House Commission on Aviation and Security: The DOT Status Report* (Washington, D.C.: U.S. Department of Transportation, February 1998).

18. Ibid.

19. Gerald L. Dillingham, "Aviation Safety and Security," *Statement to the Subcommittee on Aviation, Committee on Commerce, Science and Transportation, U.S. Senate* (Washington, D.C.: GAO Distribution Center, March 5, 1997).

20. Stuart Matthews, "FSF Disapproves of Costly Security Effort to Improve an Already Effective Safety System," news release (Alexandria, Va.: Flight Safety Foundation, July 17, 1997).

21. Flynn.

22. Carole A. Shifrin, "Potential of Explosives Focuses Renewed Attention on Security," *Aviation Week & Space Technology*, August 5, 1996, p. 34.

Chapter 7. Air Safety in Perspective

1. National Aeronautics and Space Administration, "Super Jumbo Jet Concept Would Carry 800 Passengers," fact sheet (Hampton, Va.: NASA Langley Research Center, July 1997).

2. Otto Johnson, ed., *Information Please Almanac* (Boston and New York: Houghton Mifflin, 1997), p. 406.

3. Al Gore et al., "Final Report to President Clinton," *White House Commission on Aviation Safety and Security*, February 12, 1997, <http://www.aviationcommission.dot.gov/212fin~1.html> (March 22, 1999).

Further Reading

Cole, Michael D. *TWA Flight 800: Explosion in Midair.* Springfield, N.J.: Enslow Publishers, Inc., 1999.

Gero, David. *Flights of Terror.* Sparkford, England: Haynes Publications, Inc., 1996.

———. Military Aviation Disasters. Sparkford, England: Haynes Publications, Inc., 1998.

Lopez, Donald S. *Aviation: A Smithsonian Guide.* New York: Macmillan, 1995.

This is a richly illustrated history of aviation, including commercial aviation. Its focus is on technological development.

Yenne, Bill. *The World's Worst Aircraft.* New York: Marboro Books, 1990.

This is a large-format book with descriptions and photos of airplanes that became famous because they were so bad in one way or another. Some of these failures affected later aircraft development.

Internet Addresses

Many of the documents cited in this book are available on the Internet. Here are some main sources of on-line information:

Gore Commission

<www.aviationcommission.dot.gov>

The White House Commission on Aviation Safety and Security has had a big impact on air safety efforts. Its final report is, and related documents are, available on line.

Federal Aviation Administration

<www.faa.gov>

The FAA keeps a wealth of documents and reports on line. It also has a very effective search tool for looking up aviation-related information.

National Aeronautics and Space Administration

<www.nasa.gov>

NASA works with the FAA, Defense Department, and universities to research air safety issues.

National Transportation Safety Board

<www.ntsb.gov>

Volumes of information about transportation accidents are available, including photos and animations related to TWA 800, KAL 801, and other recent crashes.

More Web sites for information, graphics, and games:

National Air and Space Museum

<www.nasm.edu>

Information about exhibits and programs. Information and colorful graphics on how things fly.

Women in Aviation International

<www.wiai.org>

Information about famous women aviators and aviation career opportunities for women.

Index

H22S12564

363.12
GAF   Gaffney, Timothy R.

            Air safety

DUE DATE BRODART 03/00 19.95			